Gender, Ethnicity and Sexuality in Contemporary American Film

JUDE DAVIES AND CAROL R. SMITH

KEELEUNIVERSITY**PRESS**

© Jude Davies and Carol R. Smith, 1997

Keele University Press
22 George Square, Edinburgh

Typeset in Monotype Fournier by
Carnegie Publishing, Lancaster and
printed and bound in Great Britain
by the Cromwell Press, Melksham

A CIP record for this book is available
from the British Library

ISBN 1 85331 174 X

The right of Jude Davies and Carol R. Smith to be identified
as the authors of this work has been asserted
in accordance with the
Copyright, Designs and Patents Act 1988

Dedication: *For Our Parents*

Contents

Acknowledgements

We would like to thank King Alfred's College of Higher Education for research grants which enabled the preparation of parts of this book.

We owe a debt of gratitude to our colleagues at King Alfred's College, especially those in the School of Cultural Studies and, in particular, Alasdair Spark, Head of American Studies. We would also like to thank the students who took our course on contemporary Hollywood on the American Studies programme in 1996.

Finally, many thanks to George McKay for helping to initiate the project and to Nicola Carr for helping to bring it to fruition.

Introduction: The Uses of Identity in Post-Reagan Hollywood Film

[An] insistence on 'positive images' ... obscures the fact that 'nice' images might at times be as pernicious as overtly degrading ones, providing a bourgeois facade for paternalism, a more pervasive racism.

> Robert Stam and Louise Spence, 'Colonialism, Racism and Representation' [1]

While the movement away from demeaning stereotypes into a larger field of cultural representation has the potential for counterhegemonic effects, mainstream cinema reveals, for the most part, a disturbing reliance on narrative structures that foreground the bourgeois ideal as symbol of racial egalitarianism. In this sense, such representations transform historical demands for civil rights into images of class homogeneity – an ideological response to radical discourses of the 1960s that reiterates what Houston Baker calls, in another context, 'AMERICA as immanent idea of boundless, classless, raceless possibility'.

> Robyn Wiegman, 'Black bodies/American commodities: Gender, race and the bourgeois ideal in contemporary film'.[2]

This book is not about the representation of various groups of Americans, defined in terms of gender, ethnicity and sexuality. Instead, we are concerned with the uses of cinematic images of identity. With reference to representations of identity and identity politics, the production and consumption of Hollywood movies have undergone substantial developments since the presidency of Ronald Reagan. In terms of production, this period has seen considerable penetration of non-white, non-straight, and non-male filmmakers into the Hollywood mainstream, while increasing market segmentation and sectionalisation of audiences have problematised the very notions of 'mainstream' and its other, the margins. A measure of these shifts was indicated in 1992 by Spike Lee's appeal to prominent African Americans to fund the completion of *Malcolm X*. The issue and its context attracted controversy; but what would have been almost unthinkable even as recently as the 1980s was that a major studio was prepared to spend as much as $18 million (out of a total original budget of $26 million) on a biopic of a black separatist icon.[3] Although Lee and others have complained rightly that African American directors find it difficult to obtain blockbuster-level budgets, the early 1990s have seen films directed by African Americans and other non-whites distributed much more widely and in greater numbers than ever.

So far as representations of African Americans are concerned, 1990s films have presented racial identity in two major ways. Directors such as Matty Rich, John Singleton, Mario Van Peebles, Joseph Vasquez, Robert Townsend, Leslie Harris and others have told narratives of cultural and racial specificity in which blackness tends to be presented as constitutive of a social and cultural context.[4] At the same time, performers such as Whoopi Goldberg, Denzel Washington, Danny Glover, Wesley Snipes and Eddie Murphy have played screen roles which, rather than being defined exclusively by essentialist constructions of ethnicity and gender, employ their cultural resonances in a variety of directions. The latter modes of representation are, in many respects, new developments, but what is perhaps still more striking is that both modes are produced side by side in many films, of which those of Spike Lee are some of the most prominent, though by no means the only, examples. Cinematic cultural space has been created in which African Americans and other non-white performers are presented in specific ethnic terms while also inhabiting centralised narrative and identificatory positions.

Crossovers into mainstream Hollywood by other traditionally marginal groups are apparent in the increasing number of women directors and in the increased visibility of multiple kinds of male homosexual identity and, to a lesser extent, lesbian identities on screen. Simultaneously, some of the more overtly patriarchal and white supremacist images of the Reagan era have become poor box office. Yet these various developments have not necessarily corresponded with economic equalisation, nor have they necessarily served to enhance the status of non-white, non-patriarchal, or non-straight cultural production. This book is aimed not at negating the importance of these developments, but at gaining a critical understanding of them.

While, as our opening quotations imply, the major focus of criticism in this field has been on representations of race and ethnicity – perhaps because of the obviousness of the historical failure to translate visibility into cultural and economic status – comparable issues are raised in regard to other modes of identity such as gender and sexuality. In all these fields, while increased visibility in what passes for the cultural mainstream has played a part in destabilising the former affiliations of identity politics, Hollywood films have also disseminated explicit discourses concerning identity, conceived in terms of race, ethnicity, gender, sexuality and generation. Contemporary viewers have become increasingly familiarised with discourses of identity that have developed in and around film, which mediate its production and consumption. The term 'talkies' has been re-coined to describe films such as *Falling Down* (Joel Schumacher, 1993), *Disclosure* (Adrian Lyne, 1994) and *Malcolm X* (Spike Lee, 1992) which explicitly engage with debates around multiculturalism, gender and ethnicity as part of their marketing and, therefore, as part of their consumption. Such movies deliberately court controversy, or at least discussion, by engaging with politicised forms of identity, and their consumption is mediated by articles and cover stories in newspapers and magazines, by television entertainment news, and, if the story is big enough, on prime-time news. Not only 'talkies,' but films as diverse as *Pretty Woman* (Garry Marshall, 1990), *Ghost* (Jerry Zucker, 1990), *Forrest Gump* (Robert Zemeckis, 1994), *Philadelphia* (Jonathan Demme, 1993) and *Glory* (Edward Zwick, 1989), all discussed in this book, make use of constructions of identity deriving from more or less politicised discourses in order to secure a variety of effects. It is a fair assumption then, that, to some extent at least, cinemagoers consume these films through the discourses of identity politics, focused more often than not on the filmic personae of certain performers.

An excellent critical response to developments in Hollywood in the late 1980s and 1990s is Tania Modleski's *Feminism Without Women: Culture and Criticism in a 'Post-feminist' Age*. Modleski takes up a rethinking of identity representations in order to launch a critique of the appropriation in representations of masculinity of feminine-gendered attributes and positions.[5] Because Modleski broadly accepts psychoanalytical explanations for identity construction, which install the gender binary as its foundation, she construes 'post-feminism' as central to post-modernist notions of dispersed subjectivity. Arguing persuasively against commentators who prematurely celebrate the de-essentialising of gendered characteristics, Modleski privileges gender as the master-code of identity representation in popular culture. Her accounts analyse the intersection of notions of identity predicated on gender, race and sexuality in recent mainstream films, while her use of the Freudian notion of disavowal enables her to ground a thoroughgoing critique of pa-triarchy, racism and homophobia. For Modleski, developments in the late 1980s in the representation of gender, including appropriations of femininity and feminism, posed difficulties for cultural critics by presen-ting them with ambiguously coded and empowered images. The result of this, as she put it, was that 'the inability to "decide" on the ideological slant of a given representation is endemic to *much* recent cultural critic-ism'.[6] Conversely, the notion of disavowal enables Modleski to demonstrate how such ambiguous representations may ultimately be subject to recuperative patriarchal and colonialist strategies. However, useful and, in Modleski's hands, incisive as this approach is, our feeling is that a Freudian insistence on finding patriarchal disavowal everywhere as a determinant structure is too reductive a critique of Hollywood multiculturalism, since it fails to come to terms with the variety of transactional uses made of racialised, gendered, and sexualised identity in more recent Hollywood films. In particular, while Modleski's invoc-ation of the psychoanalytical gender binary as a master-code does allow her to erect bitingly perceptive critical positions, it simultaneously closes down plural readings, and a sense of these is especially important, given the multiple uses to which 1990s films have put constructions of identity.

The uses of femininity described by Modleski constitute an example of Hollywood's appropriation of discourses of identity politics in order to smooth over the multiple and overlapping codes of identity through which real subjects are constituted. While Modleski is concerned with the de-essentialising of gendered characteristics, Robyn Wiegman, in another perceptive analysis of Hollywood's uses of the discourses of identity politics in the 1980s, points to the erasure of history carried out in representations of African American women. Building on feminist work which has unmasked the strategies by which other categories of oppression are rendered invisible through the image of the white, hetero-sexual, middle-class woman, for whom 'gender is the *only* means of cultural disempowerment', Wiegman demonstrates how 'positive' images of African American women in films such as *Mahogany* (Berry Gordy, 1975) and *Lethal Weapon* (Richard Donner, 1987) work in the service of hegemonic power relations.[7] By inscribing what she calls 'the bourgeois ideal' as symbol of racial egalitarianism:

> Such 'positive' images of black women are ... mediations for a reconstruction of hegemonic power, offering – through the very visibility of black female inclusion – a seemingly nonhierarchical culture in which all political and social interventions can be contained through a discursive nod to 'you've come a long way.'[8]

Critics such as Modleski and Wiegman have shown how films have worked to erase histories of oppression and to camouflage persistent power relations by de-essentialising and de-historicising gender and race. While, as will be shown later, many recent Hollywood films continue to utilise these strategies, the developments outlined above have, we argue, intensified what Wiegman calls 'the intersecting, contradictory, and cross-category functioning of U.S. culture',[9] and have produced new and different appropriations of identity politics. We will be outlining some of these in detail in the rest of this book. One of the major developments discernible is that the 'bourgeois ideal', seen as the dominant model of inclusiveness for the films that Wiegman discusses, has lost prestige, such that in many films it is represented as dysfunctional. Instead, identity is increasingly represented in terms of individuated ethnicity, gender or sexuality, according to models drawn from some elements of the traditions of identity politics. At the same time, representations such as Denzel Washington's role in *Philadelphia* demonstrate that the crossover of racially 'marginal' figures into the mainstream has now come to function in turn with respect to other kinds of marginality (in this case, of course, male homosexuality). Thus, while the appellation of a coherent and normalised identity remains present in many films, recent Hollywood movies also court ambiguous and incomplete audience identifications, so as to appeal to several audiences simultaneously and to engage with individual audience members in multiple ways.

What are the implications of these shifts and related political developments? Modleski's book and Wiegman's article stand squarely in the tradition of critical work which positions itself as decoding or unmasking the strategies of the filmic representation of identity which are held to be mystifying. Whether or not they have been firmly committed to

structuralist methodology, even the most populist of film critics have
tended to take for granted Roland Barthes's understanding of codification and culture. 'The reluctance to declare its codes', according to
Barthes, 'characterises bourgeois society and the mass culture issuing
from it: both demand signs which do not look like signs.' [10] Subsequent
critics have tended to adopt a similar model while inserting qualifiers
such as 'dominant', 'white', 'Anglo', 'European', 'patriarchal', 'heterosexual' and others in the place of, or in addition to, Barthes's 'bourgeois'.
The question posed by cinema that demonstrates a self-consciousness
about political discourses of identity, is how to handle representations
that work both as naturalisations of more or less highly politicised
identity ('this is how things – men/women/blacks/whites ... – are')
and also continue to perform symbolic or transactional functions.

Hollywood's appropriation of discourses of identity politics prob-
lematises critical discourses predicated on the unmasking of filmic codes
or ideologies, even when, as in recent work by Douglas Kellner, these
have been subjected to revisionism via theories of gender, race and
power. Kellner has argued for a multiperspectival ideological critique
which retains from Marxian theories of ideology a focus on the relations
between culture and economic power, while incorporating emphases
and analysis from feminism, psychoanalysis, and theories of ethnicity
and race.[11] In 'Film, politics and ideology: Toward a multiperspectival
film theory', Kellner first launches a project of the critical unmasking
of dominant ideology (as articulated in *Top Gun*: Tony Scott, 1986),
and then goes on to argue for the supplementation of classical Marxian
notions of ideology by attending to both internal conflict within articulations of the dominant ideology and also to contestations of the
dominant ideology from 'progressive' political interventions. In a clear
and persuasive formulation which owes a larger debt to feminist criticism
than Kellner acknowledges, he asserts that:

> Although demystification is part of ideology critique, simply exposing
> mystification and domination isn't enough ... Furthermore, on this
> model, ideology criticism is not solely denunciatory and should seek
> socially critical and oppositional moments within all ideological
> texts.[12]

However, it is difficult to see how the multiperspectival critique that
Kellner goes on to outline could cope fully with the films under discussion here. The cultural theory described in the latter part of the

article retains a narrow definition of ideological analysis as unmasking the transcodings performed by dominant or emergent ideologies. Kellner takes for granted the stability of the codes themselves, leaving demystification – the unmasking of ideological transcodings – as the be-all and end-all of formal analysis. This analysis is then supplemented by strategies such as contextualisation and relational reading, which in Kellner's definition remain fairly static operations.

The limitations of this approach can be seen in Kellner's reading of masculinity in *Top Gun* and *Rambo: First Blood Part II* (George P. Cosmatos, 1985). For him, both films directly transcode national and political issues onto representations of masculinity. These in turn function to naturalise and to validate certain political positions. Thus:

> *Top Gun*'s ideological project is to invest desire in the figure of heroic fighter pilots and high-tech war ... During an initial *Top Gun* training session, one pilot whispers to another, when watching a video of a high tech explosion/kill, 'this gives me a hard-on.' Indeed, this is the project of the film itself which turns on the spectator to the thrill of technological death, fusing eros and thanatos, libidinal energy and destruction, in images of technowar, thus helping to produce the psychological disposition to thrill to images of technodeath in events like the Persian Gulf war.[13]

At this point in the argument, Kellner seems to view the ideological workings of the film as relying on a master code of phallic masculinity in order to validate its politics. A few pages later, however, his position has subtly changed: '*Top Gun*'s conservatism is seamless and total: the film perfectly reproduces the conservative discourses of the period on winning and individual competition, the military, gender and heterosexual coupling, the family, patriotism and race.' [14] Now the potency of *Top Gun* is claimed to lie in its integration, its construction of various conservative codes as mutually reinforcing. Left unresolved by this shift in argument is the relative status of different codes. While, as Kellner states, 'demystification ... isn't enough', his definition of the job of the film critic – 'to decode their ideological messages and effects' – continues to assume the stabilities of the codes themselves.[15] In this critical position, there is no possibility of accounting for a sense of the instability of codes of, for example, masculinity.

Thus, though Kellner commends an attention to the fissures, faults and excesses in articulations of dominant ideology, he scarcely mentions some which are, as it were, under his nose. Only in an underdeveloped few lines just before his concluding paragraphs does Kellner begin to consider the critical potential of analysing *Top Gun* and *Rambo* as being 'about' masculinity, and even here he seems unaware of the possible deconstructive power of such an emphasis. To be fair, *Top Gun*, unlike the films discussed in Chapter 1 below, does not explicitly engage with debates over masculinity. Yet, in spite of his characterisation of *Rambo* as 'an exercise in conservative ideological masturbation', Kellner's account precludes the potentially destabilising effects produced by the excessiveness of representations of extreme masculinities in both films.[16]

Hollywood multiculturalism of the 1990s also puts at stake critical positions predicated on traditional versions of identity politics, which have worked by protesting negative images and campaigning for positive ones. As our opening quotations imply, such critical positions were already being debated within the contexts of identity politics and cultural studies well before these developments. In an allied move, Cornel West identified a kind of cultural production by African Americans at the beginning of the 1990s that defined itself outside notions of positive images.[17] Meanwhile, political developments such as the Hill/Thomas controversy and Bill Clinton's deliberate courting of middle-class blacks alongside a perceived neglect of working-class voters and an explicit hostility to rap culture have provoked some interventions aimed at transforming African American politics. In this context, Manning Marable has argued that the post-civil rights demand to see 'a black face in a high place' now fails to get to the heart of racial politics or the politics of racial representations.[18] At the same time, activists concerned with sexuality have also made highly visible attempts to transform an identity politics predicated on a separatist/integrationist binary. Organisations such as Queer Nation and ACT UP have explored strategies other than demanding equal status with the mainstream.

For critics and commentators such as West, Richard M. Merelman and Colin MacCabe, the emergence of African American filmmaking in the late 1980s and early 1990s, emblematised by Spike Lee, was, in itself, a pivotal moment requiring a revisionist critical apparatus.[19] Among the objectives of such a project must be an understanding of the relation between the partial penetration of Hollywood by hitherto marginalised groups and developments within mainstream forms. The interest in fragmentary and unstable identity that developed outside mainstream representations in the late 1980s and early 1990s is now discernible in Hollywood productions. While liberal 1980s films invested in a model of integration to smooth over difference – and, wittingly or not, reinscribed white patriarchal power – more recent films have employed more complex and overlapping constructions of identity. To oversimplify: along with certain historical and political exclusions, until the early 1990s the dominant Hollywood form aimed at synthesising Americanness out of the multiple and overlapping codes through which the identity of real subjects was constructed. More recently, some mainstream movies are less interested in resolving difference than in playing off overlapping codes. Previously, a major project of criticism was to expose the bogusness of Hollywood representations of integration – equality, community, and national identity; this must now be supplemented by the task of unpacking multiple representations of separatism and inclusiveness.

The films analysed in this book construct a variety of models of identity and nationality. Some, like *Philadelphia*, work partly by appealing to a liberal notion of inclusiveness in ways similar to those described by Wiegman. But others, from *Falling Down* to *Malcolm X*, employ alongside one another discourses of identity predicated on separatism *and* inclusiveness. Viewers of contemporary Hollywood movies are faced with a series of competing narratives in which representations of marginal identity are weighted not only with essentialist identity (Denzel Washington as Malcolm X), but also with symbolic roles as mediators (Whoopi Goldberg in *Ghost*, Washington again in *Philadelphia*). And while non-white roles have sustained these multiple functions, the middle-class white male is no longer assumed to occupy neutral territory. Comparable complicated multiple and partial identifications are solicited by roles such as the low IQ hero Forrest Gump and in not-quite-centred white males of the kind frequently portrayed by Michael Douglas. At the same time as hitherto marginalised identities have been partially brought into the mainstream the autonomy and the transparency of powerful white males have been represented as being in crisis.

In order to understand these structurally ambiguous and sometimes complicated negotiations, it is necessary to consider the relations between representations across a variety of genres and filmic contexts, while being aware that the films themselves solicit audience identification on a partial and ambiguous basis. Therefore, each chapter of this book focuses on a specific category of identity to consider its relations with other categories in exemplary films. Before going on to do this, however, we will exemplify the argument made above by examining a film which is pivotal between integrationist and multiple forms.

A brief reading of *Pretty Woman* (Garry Marshall, 1990) in the context of Hilary Radner's highly perceptive essay on the film in *Film Theory Goes to the Movies* [20] can be used to exemplify its pivotal status. In the opening scenes of the film, Richard Gere is shown full length and is contextualised with respect to other people, while the first shots of Vivian, the character played by Julia Roberts, frame parts of her body, her lower torso, her legs zipped into black plastic boots. In classically Mulveyan terms, the camera presents masculinity for audience identification as complete, social subject, while offering up the female body for voyeuristic pleasure, objectifying that body not merely through the voyeuristic gaze but also through a direct representation of fragmentation. Apparently, then, *Pretty Woman* initially reinscribes the Freudian power relations of the cinematic gaze as understood by psychoanalytic film theory. However, as Hilary Radner has pointed out, the film offers various pleasures to female viewers by narrativising Vivian's progress from 'voyeuristic object' to 'fetishistic object', arguing that: '*Pretty Woman* investigates that process by which the woman might become the fetish, to control the gaze of the male (rather than being controlled), earn money, and carve out for herself some small arena of private pleasure.' [21] Radner demonstrates persuasively how *Pretty Woman*, by its invocation and manipulation of the cinematic gaze, rearticulates for 1980s audiences the rewriting of consumer capitalism for a female consumer which was associated with Helen Gurley Brown and *Cosmopolitan* magazine in the 1960s.[22] What we are interested in unpacking here are two elements of the film that are given little or no attention in Radner's account: its uses of masculinity and ethnicity.

Exemplary so far as it goes, by concentrating exclusively on the relation of *Pretty Woman* to notions of (white) female identity, Radner forecloses discussion of the transactional and symbolic ways in which the film uses constructions of identity at the level of the representation of women. *Pretty Woman* can be seen to juxtapose two gendered narratives. One is the primary story of the 'pretty woman', Vivian, who begins the film as a prostitute and obtains both financial independence and a long-term relationship with the man of her dreams. But *Pretty Woman* also provides a masculine narrative which parallels this female one. Focusing on Edward, played by Richard Gere, the film plays out certain anxieties to do with masculinity and Reaganite economics which are intertwined by the secret of Gere's wealth. Instead of pursuing the traditionally manly activity of production, Edward is an asset-stripper, a morally and economically suspect mode of wealth generation. As Vivian remarks, 'We both screw people for money.' During the course of his relationship with Vivian, Edward reinvents himself as a productive male. Having come to Los Angeles to break up a company for profit, he decides instead to reinvest and enable it to make ships.

Radner does briefly mention this narrative of male transformation, but views it as functioning solely to authenticate Vivian's narrative and, in particular, as a sign of her redemption, 'her "goodness," her worthiness, and her right to wife-status and legitimacy'.[23] We would suggest also that, with a little interpretative pressure, it is possible to see the displacements of *Pretty Woman* working in the reverse of this direction, so that the redemption of Gere's masculinity is dependent on assumptions of the goodness of Roberts's femininity, which itself can never be doubted. Thus the narrative of masculine redemption is predicated on an identification of femininity with a moral attitude to money, and with Roberts as embodying throughout an integrity lacking in the financially comfortable atmosphere in which Gere is accustomed to move. In these terms, rather than Edward's redemption authenticating Vivian's 'progress', the romance narrative of *Pretty Woman* works ultimately to authorise a moral view of finance and to redeem a potentially corrupt class and gender. In sum, then, the film achieves a moralisation of Reaganite economics. It does this via a process of symbolic displacement whereby the problem of corporate raiding is rewritten via a romance narrative itself dependent on a naturalised notion of redemptive femininity. The satisfactions of this macro-economic narrative may well remain at an unconscious level for many audiences. Nevertheless, although the familiar characterisation of *Pretty Woman* is that of a film directed at females, it was consumed succcessfully not only as a chicks' movie but also as a date film.

While in terms of this two-way displacement, *Pretty Woman* looks forward to the films discussed later in this book, in other ways it continues to work along the lines of conventional Hollywood representations and repressions. For one, the camerawork does not always reiterate what Radner claims (in a passage quoted above) is Vivian's progress from voyeuristic object to fetishistic object. During the scene when Vivian shops successfully on Rodeo Drive, the camera positions viewers to enjoy Vivian's (clothed) body, even while the narrative solicits the pleasures of vicarious consumption. Possibly still more telling is the film's representation of race, which functions silently to guarantee the symbolic displacements just discussed which are predicated on gender.

While *Pretty Woman* explicitly marks itself as predicated on a gender binary, it remains virtually homogeneous in its whiteness. Non-whites are conspicuously absent from the film. In a scene-setting exchange early on, Vivian and her Italian American room-mate Kit discuss the death of a fellow-prostitute known as 'Skinny Marie', who has been murdered and dumped in a trashcan before the film's action begins. Radner acknowledges the symbolic function of this dead prostitute as embodying literally the visual dismemberment undergone figuratively in the early sequences by Vivian/Roberts:

> Vivian is not [...] 'Skinny Marie', whose death at the beginning of the film signals the difference between the position of voyeuristic object that she initially occupied – in which death would have been her inevitable reward – and the position she now occupies as fetish object. [24]

What Radner does not mention, and which the film fails to make explicit, is the ethnic or racial identity of Skinny Marie. Nevertheless, she is positioned as non-white by the logic partially identified by Radner: while in terms of gender identification Skinny Marie's body is, as Radner points out, a warning of Vivian's vulnerability, at the same time Vivian/ Roberts's whiteness always already protects her. The star status and the screen persona of Julia Roberts surely pre-empt for most audiences any anticipation of Vivian's early demise, in ways which for a variety of reasons (the persistence of white-centred formal conventions and racialised typification of female screen personae; the comparative rarity of non-white stars of Roberts's status) no non-white actress of comparable age could emulate. Especially given the statistical probability that, in real life, a prostitute in this part of Los Angeles is most likely black or Latina, Roberts's whiteness functions as an invisible protective aura. The film sanitises itself by repressing this racial distinction, partly because for the romance to work Vivian/Roberts's 'progress' or development through the film has to be seen as due to her personal qualities. Otherwise, after all, the inner nobility which dictates such ideal bourgeois responses as weeping at the opera is liable to be read as being determined by her ethnicity. Marie's 'blackness' is thus implied but not acknowledged by the film, in order that it can function to guarantee the universality of white representations of the gender binary, and thereby to authenticate the story of the 'pretty [white] woman' and the wealthy [white] man.

What *Pretty Woman* does then is to adopt a strategy of racial repre-sentation whereby difference functions to generate meaning – whiteness is associated with privilege and survival – while repressing the 'other' term which serves to authenticate these associations. While the film's construction of gender works, as we have argued, in two directions, the film as a whole still solicits responses based on holistic identities. (Perhaps the frequent references to its own fictionality underwrite this.) [25] The films to be discussed later sometimes also adopt strategies whereby otherness is repressed, but in general they are concerned with making it explicit. It is these strategies that we will be analysing in subsequent chapters.

As is clear from this brief reading of *Pretty Woman*, patterns of repression, cross-referencing, substitution and transcoding undercut classifications of films based on their thematics. Attempts to divide up Hollywood films under headings such as gender, ethnicity and sexuality run the risk of oversimplifying the overlapping and multidimensional ways in which these definitions of identity are constructed. It is therefore impossible, or at least ill-advised, to try to arrange films under headings of what they are 'about' (as, for example, when a film is said to be 'about AIDS', or 'concerned with the problem of black/white/female/male/gay/straight identity'), even when, as now, films are increasingly con-sumed in terms of the issues they invoke. For these reasons, the following chapters are not offered as definitive taxonomies of Hollywood repre-sentations of identity. Instead, each of them begins with a thematic overview of issues relevant to gender, ethnicity and race, and sexuality, before going on to consider the ways in which identities are constructed in some exemplary recent films. By this means, we hope to demonstrate the importance of developments in notions of identity politics in infor-ming the production and consumption of cinematic identity.

Notes

1. Robert Stam and Louise Spence, 'Colonialism, Racism and Representation,' *Screen* 24/2 (1983), p. 3; quoted in Robyn Wiegman, 'Black bodies/American com-modities: Gender, race and the bourgeois ideal in contemporary film', in Lester D. Friedman (ed.), *Unspeakable Images: Ethnicity and the American Cinema* (Urbana and Chicago: University of Illinois Press, 1991), pp. 308–28; p. 320.

2. Wiegman, 'Black bodies', p. 312.

3. According to Lee, Warner Brothers refused to put more than $18 million into what 'was *always* a $33 million film'. The budget was set for $26 million, the difference coming out of pre-selling rights for distribution outside the USA. For the account of wrangles over the budget for *Malcolm X* and their eventual resolution, see Spike Lee with Ralph Wiley, *By any means necessary: The trials and tribulations of the making of Malcolm X* (London: Vintage, 1993), pp. 23, 31–2, 122–3, 165–6. Lee's work is discussed further in Chapter 2 below.

4. For a not unreflective consideration of the 1991 boom in African American film-making in the context of positive images, see John Leland, with Andrew Murr, Mark Miller, Farai Chideya and Abigail Kuflik, 'New jack cinema enters screening: With 19 films this year, Hollywood fades to black', *Newsweek*, 10 June 1991, pp. 50–2.

5. See Tania Modleski, *Feminism Without Women: Culture and Criticism in a 'Post-feminist' Age* (New York and London: Routledge, 1991), p. 7 and passim.

6. Modleski, *Feminism Without Women*, p. 162. Emphasis in original.

7. Wiegman, 'Black bodies" pp. 310, 312.

8. Wiegman, 'Black bodies', p. 312.

9. Wiegman, 'Black bodies', p. 309.

10. Roland Barthes, (trans. Stephen Heath) *Image Music Text* (London: Fontana, 1977), p. 116.

11. See Douglas Kellner and Michael Ryan, *Camera Politica: The Politics and Ideology of Contemporary Film* (Bloomington: Indiana University Press, 1988), and Douglas Kellner, 'Film, politics and ideology: Toward a multiperspectival film theory', in James Combs (ed.), *Movies and Politics: The Dynamic Relationship* (New York and London: Garland, 1993), pp. 55–92.

12. Kellner, 'Film, politics and ideology', p. 73.

13. Kellner, 'Film, politics and ideology', pp. 60–1.

14. Kellner, 'Film, politics and ideology', p. 65.

15. Kellner, 'Film, politics and ideology', pp. 73, 70.

16. Kellner, 'Film, politics and ideology', p. 66.

17. Cornel West, 'The new cultural politics of difference', in Russell Ferguson, Martha Gever, Trinh T. Minh-ha, and Cornel West (eds), *Out There: Marginalization and Contemporary Cultures* (Cambridge: MIT Press, 1990), pp. 19–36.

18. Manning Marable, *Beyond Black and White: Transforming African American Politics* (London & New York: Verso, 1993), p. xii.

19. In addition to the West essay quoted above, see Richard M. Merelman, *Representing Black Culture: Racial Conflict and Cultural Politics in the United States* (New York and London: Routledge, 1995), especially Chapter 4, 'Is Spike Lee "Doing the Right Thing?"': Film as black cultural projection', pp. 97–128; and Colin MacCabe, 'Foreword' in James Snead (eds Colin MacCabe and Cornel West), *White Screens/Black Images: Hollywood from the Dark Side* (New York and London: Routledge, 1994), pp. viii–ix.

20. Hilary Radner, ' "Pretty is as pretty does": free enterprise and the marriage plot', in Jim Collins, Hilary Radner and Ava Preacher Collins (eds), *Film theory goes to the movies* (New York and London: Routledge, 1993), pp. 56–76.

21. Radner, 'Pretty is as pretty does', p. 69.

22. Radner, 'Pretty is as pretty does', pp. 57–9 and passim.

23. Radner, 'Pretty is as pretty does', p. 63.

24. Radner, 'Pretty is as pretty does', p. 70.
25. Such markers include the final words of the film which explicitly connect Hollywood and dreams, and the discourse of the fairytale romance employed by Roberts and Gere.

CHAPTER I

White Masculinity as Paternity: Michael Douglas, Fatherhood and the Uses of the American Family

[T]he social and economic changes of the past two decades are beginning to call masculinity into question. The masculinity that once
believed itself to be at the pinnacle of the natural hierarchy of things
is now being slowly exposed for what it is: a subjectivity that is
organised within structures of control and authority ... For men who
were promised recognition and a secure place in the world, there lies
ahead a frightening prospect: that masculinity will be shorn of its
hierarchical power and will become simply one identity among others.

Rowena Chapman and Jonathan Rutherford, 'The forward march of
men halted' [1]

When did I have the power?

Michael Douglas as Tom Sanders in *Disclosure*
(Barry Levinson, 1994)

This chapter is not about white males and their cinematic representations, but about white masculinity as an exemplification of
constructions of gendered identity. Our project here is twofold. First,
the familiar critical operation of unmasking naturalised representations
of white masculinity, and second, to indicate and to trace the workings
of the variety of codes involved in its construction. This is to say not
only that, like all other forms of identity, white masculinity is socially
and culturally constructed, but also to emphasise the reciprocal relationship between white masculinity and other codes such as those of class,
generation and national identity as well as race, ethnicity and gender.
Historically, Hollywood representations of white masculinity have fulfilled two major semiotic functions. They have mediated the particular

identities of white male Americans, while also focusing on other cultural and social issues and identities of ostensibly universal or national scope. In great part, this simultaneous rendering of the universalising and the specific has been predicated on (and has in turn reinforced) white patriarchal power, by constructing white masculinity as a kind of default position, ostensibly lacking specificity but defining the universal in the form of the white male. For several decades academic writing on film has played a part in unmasking these strategies. While Laura Mulvey has theorised the ways in which viewing positions that are usually taken for granted are gendered, Richard Dyer has analysed the ways in which classical Hollywood constructs whiteness as racially and ethnically 'blank'.[2] Critics such as Henry A. Giroux have shown how, even in ostensibly liberal movies like *Grand Canyon* (Lawrence Kasdan, 1991), the 'filling in' of whiteness as a discrete category of racialised identity may be done in such a way as to allow whites to acknowledge the importance of race and otherness 'without having to give up their power or privilege'.[3] This constitutes an erasure of historical and structural understandings of power and privilege which works in the service of the racist politics of the new right. What we are concerned to analyse in this chapter are the varied implications suggested by the turn in many films from the late 1980s, whereby white masculinity is on the face of it firmly embodied as a specific set of codes.

The proliferation of white father-figures in films of this period has provoked critical academic and journalistic discussion which has focused on representations of whiteness and masculinity in terms of a specific, limited ethnicity and of certain gendered characteristics. Since the 'traditional' universalising forms of whiteness and masculinity had been linked with white patriarchy, these developments have been regarded as raising the possibility of disarticulating dominant and long-established androcentrism and imperialist representations of race and ethnicity. A range of commentators have related this debate to political rhetorics and cultural discourses around a 'crisis of white masculinity'. This last phrase, somewhat confusingly, references a range of political, cultural and historical constructions, from the 'angry white males', disaffected, economically and culturally disempowered and largely Midwestern voters held responsible for the Republican landslide in the 1992 mid term Congressional elections, to the notion that, in the realm of cultural representation, it is no longer possible to reconcile the specific and the universalising codes of white masculinity. Clearly, in both cases, the power and prestige of white males is perceived to be at stake. Yet the issue is wider than merely that of constructing 'positive' or indeed negative images of white masculinity, because of the semiotic uses of such representations to connote identities based on codes such as nationality and class.

As critics such as Tania Modleski and Fred Pfeil have shown (see below), the emphasis on paternity, and the proliferation of representations of white males as fathers in films from the late 1980s on, often function as relatively new strategies for reproducing white patriarchal hegemony by annexing personal qualities hitherto typed as 'feminine'. The problem for critics has been that a concentration on unmasking these strategies has tended to underplay two sets of considerations. Almost programmatically, the critical moves of unmasking and deconstruction throw into shadow the possible fragilities, instabilities and anxieties over constructions of white masculinity that are not only, arguably, the focus of subsequent Hollywood movies, but that might also provide ways of contesting hegemony. At the same time, many critics have registered a discomfort with focusing on representations of white masculinity, whether in crisis or not, since this simple emphasis tends to reinscribe the centrality of white patriarchal culture. Just as we are hardly the first to notice these problems, we have no magic resolutions. Our strategic response in this chapter is to take a trajectory from a concern with fairly straightforward discourses of positive images, to a more complex sense of the intersection of codes of identity. We have chosen to focus on films featuring Michael Douglas, since in his 1990s output Douglas has deliberately placed representations of white masculinity in relation to politicised discourses of identity. First, though, it is necessary to review the academic debate over the political valencies of the 'domesticated' white males.

From the mid 1980s onwards an increasing number of film critics have examined the intersections between constructions of identity along the lines of gender, ethnicity and sexuality. Many of these, such as Kaja Silverman's detailed, wide-ranging and sophisticated *Male Subjectivity at the Margins* (1992), situate themselves primarily with respect to classical psychoanalytic film theory, and typically they revisit and re-vision the heterosexual gender binary on which it is predicated.[4] Cohan and Hark's 1993 collection *Screening the Male* contains essays which utilise psychoanalysis, star criticism and concerns with gender, ethnicity and sexuality to unpack some of the tensions between masculinity as a condition of signification and as performance.[5] In two books edited by Pat Kirkham and Janet Thumim, a variety of critics develop positions out of psychoanalytical film criticism. Kirkham and Thumim have separated out essays by male critics into the cleverly titled *You Tarʒan: Masculinity, Movies and Men* (1993), while the more heavily theorised and self-conscious essays in *Me Jane: Masculinity, Movies and Women* (1995), are written by women.[6] These volumes seek to bridge between theoretical discussions of gender rooted in psychoanalysis and more pluralist notions of identity. Contributors to both collections take up familiar Lacanian and post-Lacanian concerns with specularity and gender, and subject them to some precise and convincing rethinking with reference to cinemas from Europe and India as well as the USA.

Other critics, while also dealing with the cinema and identity, approach film with more concern for cultural and political contexts. Concerns with masculinity and the anti-feminist backlash feature prominently in the work of Tania Modleski and Elizabeth G. Traube, both of whom examine the intersections between ethnicity, gender, sexuality, class and generation as determinants of cinematic identity.[7] The work of Susan Jeffords combines elements of both traditions. In *The Remasculiniʒation of America: Gender and the Vietnam War* (1989) Jeffords valuably treats masculinity as carrying out cultural work by displacement: discontinuities in the national self-image produced by the Vietnam War are articulated and sometimes resolved via anxieties over American masculinity. The later *Hard Bodies* (1994) reads across films and other cultural products to disclose a specific kind of masculinity associated with Reaganite politics.[8]

At the same time that masculinity has become named as a focus of these diverse brands of film theory, Hollywood movies have themselves been engaged in producing revisionist masculinities. Since the late 1980s representations of white males as domesticated, feminised or paternal have featured prominently in numerous films in a range of genres including comedies, romances, action movies and thrillers; so much so that the cultish but mainstream gangster movie as revitalised by Quentin Tarantino is about the only mode in which macho masculinity remains intact. Even here this is achieved by virtue of ironies and self-reflexivity at the level of form which renaturalises white masculinity rather than drawing attention to its performance. In the case of *Pulp Fiction* (Quentin Tarantino, 1995), it is arguable that a parodic and homophobic construction of homosexuality serves to authenticate the straight white males.

These developments have attracted much discussion, including that by Jeffords in the books indicated above. A particular focus of debate has been the significance in terms of gender politics of shifting representations of white masculinity.[9] In the passage from *Male Order* (1988) quoted at the head of this chapter, Rowena Chapman and Jonathan Rutherford link the increased visibility of white masculinity as such, along with material factors, to a crisis in the power and authority of white males. To expand their argument, it could be considered that representations of men which do not conform to traditional notions of white masculinity might play a part in destabilising patriarchal hierarchies by making visible the constructedness of ethnic and gendered identities.[10] The focus of *Male Order* is generally on representations of masculinity which do not conform to apparently hegemonic forms, for example gay men, 'new men' and black men. The implications of these representations remain very debatable, since they could well serve to signal marginal versions of masculinity in relation to which the hegemonic power of straight white forms is reconstituted. So far as representations of white masculinity are concerned, the major recent shift, attracting much comment, has been the attribution to male characters of qualities traditionally coded feminine. While Chapman and Rutherford do identify a significant shift in cultural constructions of masculinity and their effects, in subsequent Hollywood movies the increased visibility of heterosexual white masculinity in racialised and gendered terms has in general not been construed as a crisis of representation or of anything else, for either white males or anyone else. Not that it has been 'business as usual' in late 1980s and early 1990s Hollywood, but many films (for example, but not only, the 'male transformation movies' discussed below) have succeeded in presenting images of softened and domesticated white males while at the same time shoring up their hierarchical position in ways which still often feature the construction of straight white masculinity as accessing a universal perspective. It is in this context that a number of critics have identified a tendency in recent mainstream films, whereby attempts to construct revisionist representations of white males are supplemented by the invocation of patriarchal authority.

Against the view of changing constructions of masculinity as progressive, various critics, among them Donna Haraway, Susan Jeffords and Tania Modleski, have suggested that the apparently new-found fluidities of masculinity serve to enable men and male protagonists to maintain hierarchical positions by appropriating qualities traditionally regarded as feminine. In a 1993 article Jeffords identified a particular genre concerned with defining and redefining masculinity in quite explicit ways. These were what she termed the 'male transformation movies' of the late 1980s and early 1990s, from *Regarding Henry* (Mike Nichols, 1991) and *The Fisher King* (Terry Gilliam, 1991) through to *Terminator 2: Judgement Day* (James Cameron, 1991), and, we might add, *Groundhog Day* (Harold Ramis, 1993).[11] While welcoming certain aspects of these changes in representations of men, Jeffords is generally critical, quoting Donna Haraway's telling comment that ' the image of the sensitive man calls up, for me, the male person who, while enjoying the position of unbelievable privilege, also has the privilege of gentleness'.[12]

A similar argument is rehearsed by Fred Pfeil in *White Guys*. Returning to the male transformation films recognised earlier by Jeffords, Pfeil goes further in excoriating the strategic use in these movies of the acquisition of sensitivity by male protagonists in order to preserve patriarchal power. For Pfeil, the point for the heroes of what he calls the 'sensitive guy' movies of 1991 'is not finally to give up power, but to emerge from a temporary, tonic power shortage as someone more deserving of its possession and more compassionate in its exercise'.[13]

This position is further extended by Elizabeth G. Traube in her discussion of domestic men in *Dreaming Identities: Class, Gender and Generation in 1980s film*.[14] Traube shows how, in the Steve Martin vehicle *Parenthood* (Ron Howard, 1989), the trials of fatherhood are delineated as stemming from the need to balance success in the public sphere with domestic responsibilities, whereas female characters have to choose between the two, their families suffering if they choose career. By the end of the movie Gil, played by Steve Martin, is enabled to have a measure of success both at work and as a devoted and responsible father. Not only does this reinforce patriarchal power through allowing male protagonists to appropriate 'feminine' qualities, it also denies female protagonists the potential of inhabiting cross-gendered positions. Whereas Gil can have it both ways, the women of the film must sacrifice family for career, or vice versa. Thus, while the gendering of domesticity and the public sphere has been loosened, it is freed up in one direction only. For Traube, even the domestication of the male protagonists fails to sustain close inspection. As she drily points out, '*Parenthood* includes several scenes of women in the kitchen preparing, serving, or clearing up after meals, but not one man so much as lifts a dish throughout the movie.' [15] We might add that, as with many other movies in this genre, the 'domestication' of the white male protagonist is represented in terms of personal qualities rather than actions.

Traube argues that one result of this lopsidedness is that the film fails to sustain its own ideology, since its nostalgic appeal to traditional family structures contradicts the looser and more liberal notions of the family attributed by her to the film's target middle-class and upper middle-class audiences. This indicates a welcome sensitivity in Traube's account to issues of class and generation, in addition to the gender binary that structures most work on the topic of shifting masculinities. Elsewhere in *Dreaming Identities* Traube analyses the symbolic significance of representations of paternity, launching a brief but masterful reading of John Candy's performance as the eponymous hero of *Uncle Buck* (John Hughes, 1989).[16] Using a politically grounded notion of carnivalesque, Traube shows how the entrance of the disruptive, transgressive blue-collar male into a suburban, middle-class home ultimately serves to regenerate patriarchal middle-class society, while Buck himself eventually submits to the disciplines of work and marriage.

Films in the male transformation genre are diverse and many of them are capable of sustaining multiple readings. As Traube implies, very often their focus on masculinity is overdetermined by categories other than gender, for example sexuality, race and class, as well as by political or historical issues. Traube is unusual, however, going further than most critics in exploring the reciprocal connections between codes of gender, ethnicity and generation. While as this discussion has shown that in film and cultural studies there has been a major growth in work on representations of white masculinity, the majority of this work has been concerned with, in a fairly narrow sense, the politics of gender and sexuality, and/or debates over psychoanalytic models of identity construction. Such work has tended to concentrate on unpacking the significance of these representations with respect to the role, condition and identity of white American males. Where connotative or symbolic resonances of masculinity are explored, they are usually grounded in a single overdetermining category (for example Reaganomics and the Vietnam War in the work of Jeffords). Post-Reagan, the possibilities of overdetermination raised by the intersection of constructions of identity makes these films complex cultural artefacts, and raises important political questions, in particular the issue of primacy, in ways not amenable to final resolution in gender binaries or in terms of debates over the representation of white males.

This state of affairs poses tricky problems for film criticism. One response might be to try to enumerate the uses of representations of white masculinity across the board, and in relation to comparative constructions of race and gender. However, it is hard to see how such work might avoid according privileged critical status to white masculinity, reinscribing it at the centre of filmic representation. In any case, such an approach requires far more space than is available here. Instead, in this chapter we will pay attention to exemplary encodings of white masculinity around structures of paternity. Although we suggest some comparative readings across race and gender (such as those of the African American protester in *Falling Down*; the Demi Moore and Jacqueline Kim roles in *Disclosure*), the major focus here is on white masculinity, and it is intended therefore that this chapter be read in comparison with the considerations of identity representations in the rest of the book.

A focus on paternity is important for several reasons. First, as we will argue, it is possible to discern historical shifts in the representations and in the symbolic resonances of white masculinity as fatherhood, and the family structures in relation to which it is defined. These shifts have often been strategic, in that the invocation of paternity has been a means to perpetuate the authority of white males (and, in still more complex ways, black males in films such as John Singleton's *Boyz N The Hood*, 1991) at a time of the reassignation or the de-essentialising of gender characteristics. Therefore, critical attention to these constructions can function to unmask the uses of representations of paternity in naturalising patriarchal power. Second, given that the prominence of this mode of patriarchal validation is a recent development, having come about since the mid 1980s, paternalist authority lacks some of the naturalising accretions of a long movie history. Attention to paternity is therefore a profitable place to launch consideration of the transactional uses of identity representations. Third, family structures themselves are pregnant with significance at a wider social and cultural level.

A long history of constructions of national identity predicated on familial structures, from the Pilgrim Fathers to the Daughters of the American Revolution, means that all representations of the American family are to a greater or lesser extent representations of American society. In this context, representations of paternity take on a range of cultural and social significances which parallel and cross over with their immediate relation to gender politics, to sexuality or to psychoanalytic models of identity construction. It is therefore questionable how much of the power of these films derives from audience anxieties over masculinity as such. How far, instead, might audiences be using masculinity as a kind of symbolic space in which to work through issues of race, ethnicity, sexuality and, for those films discussed here, national history? Of course, in that the symbolic space of masculinity is already highly encoded, this latter mode of consumption reiterates patriarchal assumptions.

A major shift in relations between dominant constructions of masculinity can be discerned roughly alongside the loss of faith in Reaganomics in the late 1980s. Robin Wood has summarised Reaganite films as 'capitalist myths of freedom of choice and equality of opportunity, [featuring] the individual hero whose achievements somehow "make everything all right," even for the millions who never make it to individual heroism.' [17] As mentioned earlier, Susan Jeffords has connected Reaganite politics to certain types of filmic masculinity, whereby males are presented as 'hard bodies', autonomous agents free from social ties. Where families are presented in most 1980s films, they are shown as repressing individual autonomy, as obstacles to the full development of individual freedom and success, restraining entry to the economic sphere which is represented as an outside world of opportunity and fullness. Quintessentially Reaganite films such as the comedies *Risky Business* (Paul Brickman, 1983) and *Ferris Bueller's Day Off* (John Hughes, 1986) [18] featured young males striving to escape parental authority into a world of financial speculation and reward. The economic depression and insecurity that succeeded the Reagan boom has undermined the credibility of such narratives and representations. Subsequent films, starting with the male transformation movies, reverse this polarity so that, far from being stigmatised, families become screens for Americanness, and it is the public sphere that screens the oppressive and atomising effects of capitalism. Although the conditions for its formation lie in the economic developments such that white males no longer can expect financial security nor the 'wages of whiteness', this shift in polarity has no specific and total political significance, and can be used strategically in the service of a variety of ideologies of gender, economics, and ethnicity. The family as an institution is far from ideologically stable, since it is the focus of debate for feminists, sexuality theorists and others, as well as conservatives, and notions from all of these have been absorbed and redirected by Hollywood. Similarly, in terms of representation the family coalesces notions of gender, sexuality, generation and ethnicity. This means that the politics of the relations between representations of white males and families is multivalent.

By drawing attention to popular readings of star personae across films and personal histories, Richard Dyer has suggested one way of tracing these developments and their valencies which is capable of considering audiences' senses of the development of star personae over time alongside their specific inflections film by film. From the late 1980s on a series of action heroes can be seen to have domesticated their star personae in various ways: thus Steven Seagal's *On Deadly Ground* (1994) justified its action heroics via an appeal to eco-consciousness; the presence of romantic and domestic themes increased in the *Die Hard* series, which from its opening located the Bruce Willis character with respect to his wife, whose career status, narrative importance and screen exposure are far more prominent than in classic buddy-buddy action movies. Arnold Schwarzenegger provides a particularly useful example of the revitalisation of the action-hero persona by reference to domesticity and social responsibility, both of which are represented in terms of feminisation. Such negotiations of gendered identity and gendered codification are complex and yield unpredictable results. In films such as the increasingly bizarre Ivan Reitman-directed comedies *Twins* (1988), *Kindergarten Cop* (1990), and the Arnie-gets-pregnant *Junior* (1994), as well as *Terminator II: Judgement Day*, Schwarzenegger succeeded in softening and ironising his hard body persona. The embarrassing box-office failure of *Last Action Hero* (John McTiernan, 1993), with its explicit agenda of domesticating the violence of action movies alongside its representation of the 'last action hero' as, above all, a father-figure, implies some of the difficulties involved in this project. The unpopularity of *Last Action Hero* has been attributed to a variety of factors; for whatever reason, Schwarzenegger's performance as Jack Slater failed to convince audiences to consume him as both caring father and action hero.

One performer whose star persona is built on making explicit some of the contradictions and multivalencies in constructions of white masculinity is Michael Douglas. Douglas's own filmic persona inhabits uneasily both the traditional spaces of white masculinity and the domestic spaces of the transformed man, staging the difficulties of domestication and some of the frustrations of 'angry white males'. His output features a high proportion of 'talkies'; films which set out to test the limits of debate over social and cultural issues. In these films, the relations between gender, ethnicity, sexuality and generation are made more explicit than in most Hollywood films, and even thrust into the faces of the audience, courting controversy and discussion as marketing strategies. The following analysis of some constructions of relations between the white male and the family in the films of Michael Douglas is not intended to establish a coherent development or trajectory, but to explore some of the possible negotiations between representations of white masculinity and the American family that such films have explored. As it happens, the chronological sequence of the films discussed here does describe a trajectory of increasing self-consciousness about identity constructions. Later films such as the romantic comedy *The American President* (Rob Reiner, 1995) do not bear out such a development, though they do continue to make transactional use of identity representations.

In *Fatal Attraction* (Adrian Lyne, 1987), *The War of the Roses* (Danny DeVito, 1989) and *Basic Instinct* (Paul Verhoeven, 1992), Douglas played a male protagonist whose identity was defined and secured by reference to a female other. The first and third of these play out mis-ogynistic narratives in which first a middle-class American family and then Douglas's police officer protagonist are put at stake by irruptions of uncontrolled sexuality. Both films present the male protagonist as self-divided, between his erotic desires and family affiliation in *Fatal Attraction* and between his erotic desires and his sense of personal safety in *Basic Instinct*. In both, however, ultimately the destructive power of sexuality is disavowed and displaced on to the female protagonists played by Glenn Close and Sharon Stone respectively. Both films were also consumed amid a heated debate over their representations, and were received as directly screening certain identities in ideologically loaded ways. As was widely reported, the portrayal of lesbians in *Basic Instinct* was protested in terms of negative images. The Glenn Close character in *Fatal Attraction* was read as representing feminism in general, and in particular the entry of women into business careers, in a stigmatised manner. Pauline Kael was direct in her review, writing that 'this film is about men seeing feminists as witches'.[19] In neither film, though, was much distance put around these representations, which were consumed as directly putting into circulation notions of certain identities. While these films were seen as controversial, and their meanings to some extent up for discussion (for example, *Fatal Attraction* was widely touted as a good 'date' film, and a film to provoke discussion of marital [in]fidelity), identifications remained total and readings remained dependent on basic polarities, such as the rival claims on the Douglas character by his wife and mistress. The consumption of these films was therefore dominated by debates over gender roles and relations conducted in terms of direct representation, i.e. as positive/negative images. Because of this, we have little to add to already existing accounts of these films, though this should not be taken as implying that they are any less significant than those we treat at greater length.

The films to be discussed here are *Wall Street* (Oliver Stone, 1987), *Falling Down* (Joel Schumacher, 1993) and *Disclosure* (Adrian Lyne, 1994). All three employ discourses of identity strategically. In the first of these, we will show that two codes of male-male relations (the homosexual seduction and the homosocial family) at various levels of implicitness structure and give meaning to Stone's portrayal of Reaganite capitalism. *Falling Down* works differently, engaging very explicitly with politicised discourses of identity, including versions of feminism, civil rights protest, and multiculturalism, to present an unemployed protagonist desperately in need of an identity politics for white males. Finally, we will offer a reading of *Disclosure* which seeks to trace the ways in which the film invokes debates over identity (most obviously concerning sexual harassment), which are foregrounded as issues in themselves and which also provide the semiotic space to deal with anxiety over the threat to the US economy from the Pacific Rim nations.

Wall Street: Good capitalism and bad –
The all-male family vs. homosexual seduction

Wall Street figures finance capitalism through the relationship of three white males. Gordon Gekko (Michael Douglas, in an Oscar-winning performance) and Carl Fox (Martin Sheen) compete for the allegiance of Carl's son, Wall Street broker Bud Fox (Charlie Sheen). Gekko is a super-rich financial predator, while Fox is a blue-collar aircraft mechanic and union leader. While some critics such as Roger Ebert regarded the film as articulating radical criticism of capitalism or at least of the 'capitalist trading mentality', Elizabeth Traube maintains that the 'one-sided critique of capitalism' is 'void[ed] … of any critical social content'.[20] Traube points out rightly that the film's humanist appeal is actually predicated on patriarchal structures, and that a series of liberal protagonists provide antitheses to Gekko's greed while remaining within the same financial systems. She argues for the importance of personification in the film, claiming that *Wall Street* 'personifies the moral dichotomy of destructive and productive capitalism in contrastive styles of masculinity' before going on to compare the film with *Working Girl*, in which 'the dichotomy is displaced onto oppositions between unrestrained and restrained women'.[21] To supplement a concern with 'styles of masculinity', it is necessary to investigate further the film's construction of relations between men, and in particular to analyse its presentation of male–male relations and the patriarchal *family* structures which, we will show, imperfectly contain them.

The dominant and explicit structuring device for relations between men in *Wall Street* is the patriarchal American family, purged of female members. This is marked by the film's opening titles, which carry a dedication to Oliver Stone's father, a bond trader, and still more strongly by the casting of real-life father and son Martin and Charlie Sheen playing father and son in the movie. The film sets up a binary opposition between Carl Fox, the good father, and Gordon Gekko, the bad father, who takes over the filial allegiance of Bud Fox. These two father-figures obviously stand for contesting notions of social relations; the co-operative and sternly moralistic (Fox senior is willing for his son to be jailed for illegal activities carried out at Gekko's behest, in the hope that it will teach him probity), and the amoral greed of Gekko's asset-stripper. The use of the family structure to stand for a positive image of American capitalism is hardly new. Representations of the family firm have a long history in Hollywood, for reasons which are readily apparent: representations of nurturing familial relations screen out (stand in for) oppositional or exploitative economic relations, such that workers are seen to have a common interest with their own bosses, and a neutral or antagonistic relation with workers of other companies. In both *Wall Street* and *Pretty Woman*, family relations are used to mark out good productive capitalism from evil, destructive capitalism. The atomising effects of Reaganomics are represented through figures such as Gekko and Gere/Edward who carry out raids on productive workers of all classes. In the case of *Pretty Woman*, the object of Gere/Edward's predatory interest is literally a family firm; while in Stone's film Charlie Sheen as Bud Fox betrays his father by leaking secret information obtained via Fox/Sheen senior's position in an airline union. The two films ultimately work slightly differently however, since *Wall Street* proposes the all-male family as the ideal model for capitalist relations, whereas *Pretty Woman*, as we have seen, couches its recipe for regeneration in terms of heterosexuality.

In its presentation of all-male families the structure of *Wall Street* echoes that of Stone's earlier *Platoon* (1986), rendering a political issue in terms of a conflict between good and bad fathers for the allegiance of a young male played in both cases by Charlie Sheen. In both films, this allows the Sheen character to avoid responsibility, and for the polity in general to obtain a degree of absolution through them; in *Platoon*, Chris Taylor (symbolically, and controversially) for what the USA did to Southeast Asia; in *Wall Street*, Bud Fox for his involvement in predatory capitalist practices. These doubled father-figures redirect explanation to the personal, and away from underlying structures of economics or patriarchy. Rather than demanding systematic reform or revolution then, in these films regeneration comes from the actions of individuals – at the climax of *Wall Street* the livelihoods of Carl Fox and his colleagues are safeguarded, and Gekko's plans are thwarted, by the actions of Bud in collaboration with a friendly dealer. In screening what the film presents as different types of capitalism, the struggles over paternity in *Wall Street* act as a kind of master-code, displacing and domesticating its critique of Reaganomics. But even though the dichotomy of the good and the bad father is a simple one, the all-male family structures of the film are less than stable.

As Eve Kosofsky Sedgwick demonstrated in detail, through their very denial of significance to females, patriarchal structures of homosociality produce homosexual meanings that are then frequently repressed.[22] That the homoerotic sub-text of *Wall Street* nevertheless comes near to the surface is demonstrated by some comments made by Roger Ebert in the *Cinemania* review referred to above. Neatly, if unconsciously, Ebert indicates where the film's homosociality leaks out of the father–son relations prescribed at an explicit level. He comments that 'The movie has a traditional plot structure: the hungry kid is impressed by the successful older man, *seduced by him*, betrayed by him, and then tries to turn the tables' (our emphasis).

Behind the screen of paternity, then, male homosexuality appears as the master-code underlying the film's disgust at Gekko's moral corruption, so that good and bad capitalism are encoded less by contesting affiliations between good and bad fathers, than by the conflict between allegiance to good father and to (male) seducer. By the time *Wall Street* went on release audiences were used to seeing Douglas in the context of seduction: *Fatal Attraction* had appeared earlier in the same year, surrounded by personal publicity about Douglas's own sexual incontinence, often constructed in terms of 'sex addiction'. Later in the *Cinemania* review Ebert revealingly expresses dissatisfaction with Charlie Sheen's performance as Bud Fox, finding him too much of 'a babe in the woods', and going on to say that 'I would have preferred a young actor who seemed more rapacious'. Notwithstanding the (unintentional?) camp of this comment, what Ebert perceives as a false note indicates the stresses caused by the film's need to deny on one level any homoerotic desire on the part of Bud Fox, and to negate at another level the possibility of homosexual coupling that is so troubling to its structures of paternity.

Further support for the notion that a principal element of the film's master-coding is a homophobic construction of male homosexuality comes from another quality of the film noticed by Ebert; its refusal or rerouteing of heterosexual and acquisitive desire. In his reading, the film links the reductive effects of finance capitalism to the social sphere in general, so that Gekko's possessions, 'wife, family, estate, pool, limousine, priceless art objects ... are all just additional entries on the scoreboard'; and to gender relations in particular, presenting interior designer Dorien Taylor (Daryl Hannah) as one of the perks Gekko bestows upon Fox. For Ebert, the film disallows or minimises the audience's voyeuristic enjoyment of the redesigned apartment and of the sex between Bud Fox and Taylor. He argues that what he takes to be the film's stylistic rigour, which 'never allows us to luxuriate in these surroundings' and presents 'sex and possessions [as] secondary to trading, to the action' puts on screen the logic of the gambler, which is concerned primarily not with consumption but with power. The implication, not drawn by Ebert, is that in *Wall Street* finance capitalism is ultimately found wanting not because it is too materialistic but because it is not materialistic enough. More about gambling than about greed, the real problem with Reaganomics (in *Wall Street* as in *Pretty Woman*) is that it fails to produce things. It does not take much interpretative pressure to detect a master-coding behind this whereby productive and non-productive capitalisms are screened via the dichotomy between a paternal/filial familial relationship on the one hand, and a sublimated erotic relation between men on the other; a dichotomy predicated on the distinction between the all-male family based on reproduction (whose processes remain absent since Bud's mother is dead), and a sexuality assumed to be sterile.

Male homosexuality fulfils a far more negative function in *Wall Street* than does Reaganite capitalism, which can at least be cured. The sheer excessiveness of Stone's representation, as is apparent from Ebert's review, is a sign of the fragility of the film's homosocial economy. It is as if moral discourses that critiqued manipulation, betrayal and economic exploitation were insufficient to establish the bad fatherhood of Douglas/Gekko, which could only be grounded via its (homo)sexualisation.

Falling Down: Identity politics for straight white males

The rhetorics used by director Joel Schumacher to construct *Falling Down* as a movie that simultaneously particularised and universalised the condition of white masculinity have already been discussed elsewhere.[23] In an interview in the film monthly *Empire* Schumacher described the film's straight white male protagonist as 'a seemingly ordinary man ... [whose] release is so identifiable to all our angers', going on to call the script 'so representative', with 'that everyday *insanity* to it'. Yet later in the same discussion Schumacher called the same character 'one of these invisible people that we don't pay attention to ...'; an example of one of the 'many armies of men' largely ignored by contemporary American media.[24] References elsewhere in the interview to the anger articulated in films made by African Americans signalled *Falling Down* as an attempt to stake out the angst of economically and culturally dispossessed white males as a special interest group, but continual references here and in the film's publicity to its central protagonist as 'everyday guy' and 'ordinary man' sought to maintain the culturally central position of white masculinity. Here we will focus on the parallel narratives of the male figures in the film.

In summary, *Falling Down* is the story of one day in the life of Bill Foster, a.k.a. D-FENS (played by Michael Douglas), who abandons his car (registration D-FENS) in a rush-hour traffic jam and walks across Los Angeles to the house of his estranged wife which is situated in Venice. During the course of the film we learn that he has been made unemployed as a result of the peace dividend, and is intent on returning 'home' for the birthday of his daughter, for whom he can no longer provide economically. En route, D-FENS is involved in a series of scenes which crystallise urban frustrations and dangers, involving a Korean storekeeper, Latino gang members, a burger bar, an encounter with a neo-Nazi who runs an Army Surplus store, and another with a retired amateur golfer who peremptorily orders D-FENS off his territory. For much of this time, D-FENS is armed with a holdall full of guns picked up as a result of his encounter with the gang members. He is tracked across Los Angeles by the middle-aged white cop Prendergast (Robert Duvall), who arrives in Venice just in time for a climactic face-off with D-FENS. Having been subjected to practical jokes and to ridicule by his white, Asian, and Latino colleagues, and hysterical phone-calls from his wife throughout the film, on his way to Venice Prendergast punches out one of the former and takes control of his domestic arrangements. Finally he completes his redemption by shooting D-FENS dead, even though, it turns out, at this point D-FENS is armed with nothing more dangerous than a water pistol.

Critical attention was directed from the start to three examples of white masculinity in the film: D-FENS, Prendergast, and Nick, the neo-Nazi.[25] What was less often commented upon was the relation between these three and a fourth construction of masculinity, an African American protester seen briefly in a scene fairly early in the film. Wearing similar clothes to D-FENS, a white short-sleeved shirt and dark trousers, this man is picketing a bank for its racism, holding a sign saying 'Not Economically Viable', presumably after having had an application for a loan refused. As D-FENS approaches, he points to a white male leaving the bank, commenting ironically that this man must be 'economically viable'. At the close of the scene, the African American is taken away in a police car, from which he exchanges gazes with D-FENS and says 'Don't forget me.'

This scene between D-FENS and his African American other plays out a familiar trope in American culture, though with a new twist. As Werner Sollors has pointed out, 'In America, casting oneself as an outsider may in fact be considered a dominant trait.'[26] Sollors's further remark that 'Nobody wants to be a Pharisee' was echoed in a political discourse by New York University sociologist Michael Kimmel, during a discussion of *Falling Down* on CNN's news and comment *Crossfire* show. 'Nobody wants to be an oppressor,' commented Kimmel during the broadcast on Oscar night, 1993.[27]

Writing in the *Journal of American Studies*, Liam Kennedy has perceptively described this exchange as carrying out an erasure of racial identity and history:

> The gaze between the two men is presented as one of equal recognition [...] However, given the privileges accorded D-FENS' imperial vision throughout the film his gaze can only function to colonize and determine the meanings of 'blackness'. The crude liberalism motivating this scene at once idealises and negates the alterity of the black subject. More than this, it induces historical amnesia.[28]

Given that this scene is purely excessive in narrative terms, it is clear that the African American protester is there for his iconic status, figuring simply by his presence the historical oppression and protest associated with his race. Kennedy is surely right to argue that in order to enforce the parallel with D-FENS the legislative, social and cultural oppression of African Americans is elided in an act of cultural imperialism. But something is missed by readings of the representation of D-FENS and the African American protester as straightforwardly dominated by imperialist vision. First, Kennedy perhaps overplays the scene's erasure of African American history. The iconicity of the African American protester is oddly confused, not only 'idealising and negating the black subject' but also historicising it. His dress, dark trousers and white short-sleeved shirt, identify him with D-FENS, but his placard and anti-racist message locate him in the tradition of civil rights protest. By contrast, D-FENS has no sense of history, and finds himself disallowed from a politicised understanding of his own position. Moreover, while the film reproduces a distinction between African American as specific and white as universal and lacking history; the polarities have changed, since the film presents universalising discourses as having little authority in a territorialised USA.

The scene not only implies a strong affinity between the positions of the two males, cemented by their similar clothing and the look they exchange; it also, and perhaps more powerfully, suggests their differences. Historically, such pairings might have operated to allow constructions of white masculinity both a route to the privileged universal position and a connection with the authenticity of outsidership. But here this bridge is blown up, since African American 'authenticity' is explicitly constructed out of politicised discourses of identity, which D-FENS, crucially, is never allowed to use. Having been deprived (by his unemployment and divorce) of economic power and patriarchal authority, D-FENS finds that a racialised and balkanised LA is resistant to the language of disinterested moderation ('my rights as a consumer', as he says in the Korean store; and the 'honest decency' invoked by Slotnick on CNN's *Crossfire*). What had been a 'both ... and' win-win position for white masculinity becomes a lose-lose: appeals to universal values having lost authority, the unemployed white male seeks to appropriate political discourses of identity, only to find such positions already taken up and well defended.

As part of D-FENS's dysfunctional narrative, the point of this parallelism is to demonstrate that in American culture as a whole the particular condition of D-FENS is prevented from being articulated. The African American, the film implies, has a discourse developed through the struggles against racism and for civil rights which enables him to understand his oppression and to protest against it. By comparison, D-FENS has no way of understanding his own situation. Instead of being able to locate himself with respect to a history of oppression and its contestation, and/or to establish an identity with others in the same condition, D-FENS experiences his loss of job, wife, home and daughter as an inexplicable victimisation which he is powerless to resist or to put into words. At worst, then, at this level, *Falling Down* might be read as a piece of special pleading on behalf of unemployed white males, suggesting that they deserve access to discourses of victimhood, and that they will turn violent if denied it. This at least conflicts with, if not undermining completely, any demand for the rest of America to acknowledge the centrality of the white male. Furthermore, by at one level eliding social and cultural racism, the film does point to similarities between the positions of these two males in terms of economic class.

Later events in the film might also be read as presenting D-FENS as unfairly deprived of the status of victimhood determined by gender. The encounter with the neo-Nazi is in many ways pivotal: where before this scene D-FENS is presented as potentially embodying a universal resentment at common urban frustrations, afterwards his behaviour is more violent, less justified, and more directly readable as vigilantism.[29] This shift is marked by D-FENS telling his wife in a phone call before he leaves the store that he has 'passed the point of no return'. What has happened to produce this is an attempted rape and murder. Nick, the neo-Nazi, (mis)recognises D-FENS as a kindred spirit and takes him into the back room of his army surplus store. When D-FENS refuses his overtures ('I'm an American – you're a sick asshole'), Nick attempts to anally rape him. D-FENS stabs him, struggles free and shoots him dead. This scene courts readings on several levels: the problematic differentiation of D-FENS from a recognisably fascist version of white masculinity; the juxtaposition of frustrated male bonding and anal rape; the ascending order of persecutions suffered by D-FENS which now threaten to penetrate his body; and more.[30] In addition to these, by its position in the narrative, the encounter with Nick suggests that D-FENS's descent into less discriminate violence is explicable as produced by rape trauma. The incoherence of *Falling Down* is such that within the genre conventions which the film draws from vigilante pictures and westerns, such an argument is absurd, yet its tone suggests a sense of injustice that D-FENS is disallowed from benefiting from such discourses.

In some of Douglas's later films, similar appeals are consolidated into a purely self-serving articulation of white male angst in the face of persecution.[31] However, *Falling Down* does not effect this foreclosure. The film's paralleling of D-FENS with the protester, and his placement in opposition to the economically successful Prendergast, can be read as disclosing the secret truth of economic class: that it is economics rather than ethnicity which most determines power. This reading is supported by the ending of the film, in which D-FENS sacrifices himself in order to provide for his daughter via his life insurance, and Prendergast is empowered economically by the whole episode which has enabled him to prove himself as a man and a cop, and thereby to resist pressures to retire. D-FENS even adopts the African American protester's phrase 'Not economically viable' to describe himself, in his conversation with Prendergast just before his death. While this could be read as cementing the metaphorical and, as Kennedy's argument shows, illegitimate full identification of D-FENS with the unnamed protester, the dysfunctionality of the D-FENS narrative can be read ultimately as undermining this association. Certainly Michael Douglas's delivery of the line 'I'm not ... economically viable' suggests less a sense of identification with the African American figure than a wondering confusion. Unlike the African American, who is last seen being taken away in a police car, a visible symbol of the legal and physical elements of institutionalised racism (especially in Los Angeles, post-Rodney King), D-FENS literally has nowhere to go, and is unable within the terms of the film to position himself with respect to a politicised form of identity. Having set up the parallelism between white and black males who are both economically subordinate, *Falling Down* in this reading negates the possibility of full identification, because the film itself suggests that the very politicisation of discourses of identity depends on ethnicity and gender. In this sense, *Falling Down* can be read not so much as appropriating African American political history as rather partially rendering the complex political relationship between African Americans as victims of legal, cultural and economic oppression, and an unemployed white male.

In this reading, then, the representation in *Falling Down* of relations between white and African American males is nuanced in ways that are lacking in more prominently interracial buddy movies. Fred Pfeil's account of what he calls the 'proto-sexual' transactions between Riggs and Murtaugh (Mel Gibson and Danny Glover) in the *Lethal Weapon* films and McClane and Powell (Bruce Willis and Reginald VelJohnson) in *Die Hard*, identifies ways in which the white males confer on their black buddies the capacity for effective violence and 'something very like virility itself', while in exchange the African Americans curb the most excessively self-destructive violent urges of their white counterparts by dispensing '*feminine* healing'. Pfeil's account also draws attention to the provision in these films of political and historical references, 'scrambled' so as to allow identification from left- and right-populist perspectives, which contextualise and suggest links between protagonists.[32] We regard *Falling Down* as offering up a somewhat different series of connections between gender, race, history and politics. If, as Susan Jeffords argues, films such as the *Rambo* series encode narratives of national history, and specifically the Vietnam War, in terms of a narrative of white masculinity, in *Falling Down* the logic is reversed so that references to Vietnam iconography (helicopter sounds, D-FENS's homecoming as 'G. I. Joe') are used to encode a white male narrative.[33]

Openly 'about' a perceived crisis of white masculinity, *Falling Down* positions its protagonists explicitly with relation to politicised discourses of identity. This is especially true of D-FENS, the African American protester, and Nick the neo-Nazi (whose status is secured by his harassment of two stereotypical gay men who come into his shop, his harassment of a female police officer and his racist comments about 'niggers'), but the other major protagonists are also linked with political positions. Prendergast in his personal (fatherly) and professional relationships with a Latina police officer (played by Rachel Ticotin)

symbolises soft or liberal multiculturalism, while D-FENS's ex-wife
Beth (Barbara Hershey) is presented as the beneficiary of the kind of
feminism that has helped to confer on her judicial protection such that
D-FENS is prohibited from coming within a certain distance of her
(a state of affairs initially represented as ridiculous since she she cannot
quite remember the exact distance). However, these discourses are systematically and explicitly destabilised during the film's narrative: it turns
out that Beth needed the protection audiences were earlier encouraged
to resent, but Prendergast saves her anyway, finally, the dead D-FENS
elicits at least as much sympathy as the wise-cracking policeman. Further, while the negative portrayal of a Korean shopkeeper early in the
film implies a clumsy and doubly racist attempt to court an African
American audience alongside angry white males, most of the racialised
representations in the film affirm notions of political correctness. And
most importantly, as we argued earlier, the identification of D-FENS
with the African American protester is only partial. Thus the transcoding
of racialised and gendered characteristics Pfeil identified on the basis of
individuals in the *Lethal Weapon* and *Die Hard* films is impossible in
Falling Down, because in this film racial and gendered identity are always
already represented as politically constructed.

Politically, *Falling Down*'s dystopian representation of Los Angeles
(and by extension the USA) as fragmented into special interest groups
can cut in a variety of ways. On the *Crossfire* programme, Barry Slotnick's attempts to convince the panel that D-FENS stood for the feelings
of honest decent people were met with ironic laughter. But if the film
marks the problematisation of quasi-universalist discourses that privilege
white patriarchy, it envisages this problematisation apocalyptically, as
the end of the American synthesis. On the same programme, Michael
Kimmel laboured hard, with little success, to defend the cultural existence of a crisis of white masculinity while simultaneously trying to
unmask its lack of economic basis. Perhaps still more tellingly, none of
the contributors cited or defended the heritage of identity politics in
terms of equal rights legislation. Despite the programme's even-handed
appearance, both Kimmel and his liberal interlocutor Michael Kinley
instead represented identity politics according to conservative discourses
of victimhood. This suggests that even commentators who rejected the
film's androcentrism and white-centredness were unable or unwilling
to salvage a viable notion of identity politics from it. The political
implications of the film are thus unstable and ultimately up for grabs.

It is amenable to right-wing readings. However, *Falling Down* might also suggest a way forward from identity politics rather than a retreat from them: the only material determinant of identity that has any coherence through the film is economics – lack of financial power constituting the difference between the two white males D-FENS and Prendergast, and the similarity between D-FENS and the protester.

Disclosure: Virtual identities – sexual politics and Pacific Rim economics

Disclosure, directed by Barry Levinson, again features Michael Douglas playing a male protagonist undergoing some kind of crisis of power and identity which is presented as intersecting with several debated issues. Here the immediate hook for the film, exploited in its marketing (as compared with marital infidelity and feminism in *Fatal Attraction*, economic and political relations between the USA and Japan in *Black Rain* [Ridley Scott, 1989], sexuality in *Basic Instinct* and the legal and economic disempowerment of white males in *Falling Down*,) is sexual politics, and in particular sexual harassment. Douglas plays Tom Sanders, the Seattle-based head of production for computer company Digicom. Opening, like *Fatal Attraction*, with domestic scenes of the Douglas character at home with wife and family, *Disclosure* initially represents that family structure, like its precursor, as under threat from a combination of the actions of a sexually aggressive/liberated woman in the workplace (Sanders's new boss Meredith Johnson, played by Demi Moore), and Sanders's undisciplined heterosexual desire (his sexual promiscuity before marriage, which included a relationship with Johnson). In this case the Douglas character refuses the advances of Moore/Johnson, who tries to seduce him and accuses him of sexual harassment when he refuses to have full sex with her. However, sexual politics is by no means the sole or even the dominant theme of the film. The harassment narrative is resolved well in advance of the movie's climax, in fact some twenty-seven minutes before the end. The importance of sexual politics is further devalued when it is revealed that the incident was initiated by Digicom's top brass (Donald Sutherland as MD Bob Garvin, and Dylan Baker as Philip Blackburn) as part of a plot to safeguard a moneyspinning merger. The harassment accusation is a means to remove Sanders from his post so that he can subsequently be blamed for production problems in the company's Malaysian factory, problems which were actually caused by a series of cost-cutting measures initiated by Johnson, under pressure from Garvin, Blackburn, and the Malaysian government. The climax of the movie then is concerned with Sanders's successful attempt to clear himself of blame, the eventual completion of the merger, and Johnson's subsequent sacking and replacement with a middle-aged female colleague. Thus the sexual harassment narrative screens a narrative of corporate take-over. This economic narrative focuses anxieties over both internal and external challenges to the American economy: the economic and social effects of the switch away from domestic manufacturing on the one hand, and the globalisation of capital and the emergence of Pacific Rim economies on the other.

The perceived threat from Pacific Rim economies is screened at several removes. Actual Asians are screened out almost completely. The Kuala Lumpur factory is never shown directly or in realist fashion. The dominant representation of it in the film is an artist's impression on a computer screen; in addition to this the sole images are those of the factory boss Arthur Kahn on a video link, and a few brief moments of Johnson visiting the production lines, which Sanders shows on a video purportedly lifted from Malaysian television. To disavow overt racism the film provides one very unthreatening positive image: Cindy Chang, Sanders's secretary (played by Jacqueline Kim). Chang is pressurised and manipulated into giving evidence against Sanders at the harassment mediation hearing, but her unease at this is made evident at the time by her anxious and uncertain demeanour and they are quickly reconciled. The screening out of direct representations of Asians is made possible by the film's strategy of screening the Pacific Rim challenge in terms of the disruption caused at Digicom Seattle by the presence of Moore/Johnson as a sexualised woman. By this strategy of transcoding, the threat of the female other in the workplace figures the threat of Asian others in the marketplace.

Again, to disavow overt US jingoism, no-one in the movie explicitly conceptualises the friendly American buy-out of Digicom as a protective move against possible take-overs from overseas, although such interpretations can hardly be far from the minds of filmmakers and viewers who saw Japanese companies buy up Hollywood studies, film distributors and recording companies during the decade before *Disclosure* was made. The screenplay also softens at least one of the more explicitly coded references in the novel by Michael Crichton, on which it is based. The film takes over wholesale the names in Crichton's book, including that of the American company taking over Digicom, 'Conley-*White*' (our emphasis). However, in the film, references are almost always to formulations such as 'the Conley people', and only once in around twenty mentions of the firm is the full hyphenated form used (by Douglas/Sanders in conversation with his lawyer, and easily missed by viewers). The fear of the penetration of American industry by overseas capital is doubly displaced. It is first screened as a narrative of a domestic merger, and then as a sexual harassment narrative. These screenings operate therefore to transcode economic anxieties, projecting them on to the arena of sexual politics where they can be resolved – the 'bad' woman Demi Moore, whose overt use of sexuality has proved disruptive to the company, is expelled, and the less highly sexualised, more hard-working and talented (almost to the point of omniscience) Stephanie Kaplan, with student son in tow, is appointed to replace her. However, a series of explicit and implicit references to discourses associated with identity politics made throughout *Disclosure* mean that to think of the film as being 'really about' anxieties over Pacific Rim economics and somehow cloaking this in the sexual politics narrative is to oversimplify it. In what follows we will concentrate on two more aspects of the film that complicate the relationship between these screenings: first, its invocation of another set of issues concerning digital technology and identity, which mediate between the themes of economics and sexual politics, and second, the explicit merging of the narratives of economics and sexual politics in its final third, which undermines the separation necessary for the resolution-through-transcoding strategy to be successful.

Beginning with the first of these, the invocation in *Disclosure* of a series of issues concerning digital technology articulates the political and economic screenings just discussed to constructions of national identity. This is made most explicit in two set-piece speeches in this wordy film which express the upside and the downside of digital technology for notions of American identity. For the first Johnson/Moore occupies centre stage at a presentation for Digicom's new product Arcamax, some kind of portable CD-ROM player whose details are presumably kept deliberately sketchy. After a brief recital of technical specifications, she launches into an inspirational speech:

What we're selling here is freedom. We offer through technology what religion and revolution have promised but never delivered. Freedom from the physical body. Freedom from race and gender, from nationality and personality, from place and time. Communicating by cellular phone and hand held computer, PVA and built-in fax modem, we can relate to each other as pure consciousness.

Backed with some video projections which are certainly very pretty if not exactly spectacular, Johnson is offering here a notion of digital technology as a fulfilment of the American dream, articulating the discourse of America as 'boundless, classless, raceless possibility', described by Houston Baker,[34] to a futurespeak of commodified digital communication. In its exclusion of any notion of economic accessibility, and its reduction of social relations to matters of communication, the speech lowers the political horizon of such discourses as it extends their geographical scope. Nevertheless, even this deracinated version of a liberatory American teleology is not allowed to stand unqualified, and elsewhere the film evokes anxieties about the brave new world of digital technology. If technology can help to realise what *Disclosure* evokes as the enlightenment ideal of a gender-blind, race-blind, transparently organised polity, it can also frustrate the enlightenment projects of enquiry after truth and justice. Later, in a speech which negates the celebratory tone of Johnson's, Bob Garvin, MD of Digicom, insists on the impossibility of distinguishing between rival truth-claims, in this case the competing narratives of Sanders and of Johnson concerning the alleged harassment incident. Giving Sanders a lift to a reconvened arbitration session, Garvin refers to their contradictory versions of events. When Sanders contests this, arguing that his story is not a version but the truth, Garvin expatiates 'It's always somebody's version. That's the legacy of the modern age. We have information but no truth. Litttle flashes of electrons in a grain of sand.'

Johnson's earlier speech implies a subtext for this remark, which relates it to dystopian views of multiculturalism as being the fragmentation of a coherent American polity and culture into a myriad of individuals or special interest groups, each with its own specific history and interests, a notion which clearly informed *Falling Down*. Somewhat against this conservative position, however, the film's narrative associates the control of advanced technology with abuse of corporate power. The corrosive effect of digital technology on traditional truth claims is utilised by the Digicom bosses in order to implicate Sanders in the production problems in Malaysia, when Garvin and Blackburn instruct Johnson to delete all the incriminating records on the company database. In the most intense and exciting section of the film, Sanders discovers the nature of the plot against him while in virtual reality. Digicom have set up one of their show-off prototypes in the hotel room of a Conley-White executive. Called 'the corridor', this renders the whole of Digicom's records in VR. Electronically locked out of the Digicom computer, Sanders slips into the hotel room to access records on the corridor equipment. Simultaneously Johnson, back in the Digicom offices, is deleting the incriminating files. The film screens the VR images of Douglas and Moore very differently. Visually, Douglas's VR image is naturalised. He is shown in whole body, with occasional break-up at the edges as a guarantee of its authenticity. By contrast, since she is accessing the system from an ordinary pc, Moore/Johnson is depicted as a two-dimensional head and shoulders mounted on a three-dimensional outline of a female form. Her monstrosity is further emphasised by her sudden appearance from behind some files Sanders is looking at, causing him to gasp 'My God! She's in the system.'

The film's presentation of this encounter in VR reconstructs in various ways Johnson's earlier celebration of digital technology as enabling 'freedom from the physical body ... from race and gender.' Through Douglas's barely mediated body, it anchors the promised expansiveness of VR by reference to the white male body as a standard. This makes the celebration of VR look very like the pre-identity politics notions of the melting pot, whereby the motility of identity offered by the dominant ideology to non-Anglos and non-males camouflages the insistence on the centrality of WASP models. The shocked comment of Sanders/ Douglas, 'My God! She's in the system', calls down the full force of phallocentrism. In counterdistinction to the film's narrative, which has presented control of cyberspace as, threateningly, belonging to the Johnson/Garvin/Blackburn axis, suddenly the world of the computer has become Sanders's space, now under threat from female intrusion. This can only make sense through the film's invocation of the 'woman problem' narrative, whereby the space of business is assumed to be male, and thereby gender-free, and to which the intrusion of the female represents the intrusion of sexuality.

In comparison to Douglas's cyberimage, Moore's VR image constructs the loss of physicality as the loss of humanity. What exactly makes her monstrous though is more ambiguous. The scene can be construed as presenting the sexualisation of women as either natural or unnatural. On the one hand, the monstrosity of Moore's VR image could be attributed to the loss of sexuality determined by its disassociation from her actual body. On the other hand, according to the logic just outlined, VR reveals a secret truth repressed by political correctness (but at the centre of the film), that the sexualised woman is itself monstrous, especially in the workplace. It is not necessary to invoke psychoanalytic theory to construe these opposing readings in terms of fetishism and voyeurism, but we would suggest that psychoanalysis is helpful here in maintaining that this is not an either/or, but that these meanings are offered simultaneously.

At one level, the irruption of sexuality into 'the system' is how the film represents women in the workplace. The focus of this construction is of course Moore/Johnson, whose body is frequently presented for scopophilic pleasure. The first shot of Moore/Johnson is from the back as she goes upstairs, and the camera angle encourages the film viewer to follow Douglas's/Sanders's voyeuristic gaze at her legs, while a quick cut to his smiling figure serves to naturalise the fetishism involved. At this stage, Moore/Johnson is not even identified to the viewer; to him/her, as presumably for Sanders, this is just another woman. A few minutes later, still before her face has been shown or her voice heard, Moore's legs are used to frame Garvin and Sanders entering an office. Other female Digicom employees such as Mary Ann Hunter (discussed below) and Cindy Chang are by contrast de-sexualised by their clothing, appearance, age or maternity, as in the case of Stephanie Kaplan, who is strongly typed as a working mother.[35] The presence of these images of successful women, together with several internal commentaries on sexual politics, complexifies and somewhat redirects the overtly anti-feminist representation of Moore's character.

The first explicit commentary on sexual politics to appear in the film constitutes an almost classic example of disavowal in Modleski's sense. On his way to the office on Monday morning (the film is divided into daily sections) Sanders speaks to a middle-aged man on the ferry, who claims to have been made redundant ('surplused') by IBM. When Douglas gives him the card of his secretary, Cindy, the bespectacled man remarks 'Women – once you just had fun with them. Now they want your job.' As well as providing male viewers with a conservative explanation for economic distress or career blight, the articulation of this perspective allows liberals and younger viewers to distance themselves from it. Both positions are given some support by the film's narrative. The sexual harassment issue is subsequently revealed as a red herring, the pretext rather than the cause of Sanders's victimisation. Yet the near success of the plot against Sanders, and the positioning of a white male as its victim, implies that the entrance of numbers of women into business careers is not such a false explanation for middle-class male unemployment. Like Nick the neo-Nazi in *Falling Down*, this character is clearly positioned in the film to articulate an objectionably ultra-conservative position in order that the more liberal sentiments of the other characters can be thrown into relief. He therefore operates as a means of disavowal, in that he articulates sentiments that the film explicitly distances itself from, yet which remain implicit in its use of the narrative of sexual harassment to deal with anxieties over the American economy. Nevertheless, the film's narrative structure is such that the harassment narrative proves insufficient to resolve such anxieties, and is itself collapsed into the economic/merger narrative.

Another important commentary is provided by the only female member of Sanders's four-strong work group, Mary Ann Hunter (Suzie Plakson). Presented sympathetically, Hunter makes standard feminist attacks on sexual discrimination in the workplace, and scorns Johnsons's use of sexuality, instead of hard work and talent, as a means of advancement. While Hunter does make explicit a critique of the Johnson character from a certain feminist perspective, the effect of this is not necessarily to distance women in general and feminism in particular from Johnson's exploitation of legal protection for women. Instead, having Hunter onside helps to justify the representation of Sanders as white-male-as-innocent-victim of political correctness.

If, as we have argued, D-FENS in *Falling Down* is presented as lacking a discourse in which to articulate his identity, the character played by Douglas in *Disclosure* quickly learns one. While in the previous film it was the discourse of civil rights that was presented as unavailable to D-FENS, via his incomplete identification with the black protester, in *Disclosure* Sanders appropriates feminist discourses in order to formulate a language of male oppression. When he goes to consult lawyer Catherine Alvarez (Roma Maffia), she treats him to a long speech beginning 'Sexual harassment is not about sex; it is about power. She [Johnson] has it; you don't ...'. Later, at home, in conversation with his wife, Sanders gives full vent to the rhetoric of white male in crisis that *Falling Down* invokes more tenuously. When Susan (wife and career lawyer, whose status is indicated by the use of her maiden name Hendler in the closing credit sequence) suggests that he react as a woman would have done, apologise and get his job back, Sanders bursts out 'Why don't I just admit it? Why don't I just be that guy, that evil white male that you're all complaining about. I liked that; then I could fuck any-body', before calling down the (Asian) maid to exercise his 'rights'; finally, echoing Alvarez's explanation of sexual harassment as being about power not sex, he asks rhetorically, 'When did I have the power?'

Although perhaps most viewers might regard Sanders's appeal as a self-serving attempt to appropriate discourses from identity politics in support of a uniquely privileged identity – not just a white male but a white, upper middle-class, stock option-holding, married to a lawyer white male – it does echo, perversely, the call raised by feminists to distinguish between the differential power status of men.[36] In some ways, then, the corporate plot can be read as exposing bogus appropriations of some discourses of identity politics on the part of upper middle-class men and women. For example, Garvin's professions of aiming to break the glass ceiling are only a cover for shady dealings in which both Johnson and Sanders are mere pawns; Garvin and Blackburn pay lip service to eradicating sexual harassment, but only in order to remove Sanders. For some viewers, then, *Disclosure* may evoke the critiques that have been made by some feminists and African Americans of the appropriation and utilisation of positive discrimination policies by middle-class Americans, especially women.

However, the film goes further than this, going out of its way to show anti-discrimination legislation as absurd or dangerous. At one point, for example, Alvarez explains to Sanders that her marriage to a senior partner would never have come about under current legislation, since his asking her out subsequent to a first refusal would have been construed as harassment. The major difficulty in sustaining a reading of the film as critical of appropriations of such legislation rather than the legislation itself, is generated by the film's construction of race and ethnicity as a binary opposition between Asians and American whites. Cindy Chang, presented as a naturalised Asian American, may well have been especially written into the screenplay to provide an alibi for this (there is no such character in Crichton's novel). African Americans, and with them the visibility of the roots of both the discourses of identity politics and anti-discrimination legislation in the struggle for civil rights, are largely screened out of the film.

This film presents no character as a victim of sexual or racial discrimination, but it shows several people as victims of anti-discrimination legislation. Several of the latter are hard-working women who do not use sex to get on, but the major victim is a middle-class white male. Yet, ultimately, as with many of Douglas's films, what does anchor the movie's sense of values and justice is not a direct appeal to the white male as the model of probity or as embodying unproblematically a core American identity. Instead, making *Disclosure* a kind of photographic positive to the negative of *Falling Down*, Sanders is justified and sustained by his family.

In *Disclosure* the family mediates new social relations. It is not defined against digital forms of identity, but it transforms them, domesticating computer technology and economic relations alike. The film begins with a young girl, Sanders's daughter Liza, reading one of his emails at home, and it ends when Sanders reads an email in his office which says 'Daddy We Miss You. [signed] A Family', complete with assorted childish hearts, smiley face and a bunny. The Family anchors Sanders and the film. *Disclosure* contains the most explicit plea in any Douglas film for audiences to sympathise with the white male robbed of power, while at the same time using his narrative to work through anxieties based in economics and nationality. But the crucial semantic element in all the films discussed here is not white masculinity per se, but the straight white male in the context of family relations. Each of these films presents the American family as under threat from external forces; in each of them these conflicts screen anxieties about American economic performance. These anxieties are figured through representations of straight white males as fathers. But, as is clear, families function in different ways in each of the films: the all-male family as the implicit model for productive capitalism in *Wall Street*, the nuclear family as a realm of domesticity from which white males are excluded with violent results in *Falling Down*; and finally the heterosexual family in *Disclosure* as both the location of support and the justification for the centring of white males. What we have tried to make clear though, is that the discourse of the family in all of these films is neither their exclusive nor dominant concern. Instead, the family is used in different ways to screen (alternately naturalising and staging) conflicting notions of national, gendered, and racialised identity.

These symbolic links between paternity and national identity are made explicit in *The American President*, in which Douglas plays the eponymous role as a widowed father. They are stated most clearly in Robert Zemeckis's *Forrest Gump* (1994), where the heterosexual romance narrative of Forrest and Jenny structures the film's portrayal of American history since the 1960s. We regard *Forrest Gump* as legitimating white patriarchal histories of America in innovative fashion. Notwithstanding his heroism in public historical terms as a soldier, an international ping pong player, a successful businessman, an assistant at Integration and exposer of Watergate, the most moving sections of the film portray Gump as heroic, and at the same time ordinary, in his relationship with Jenny and his son. The key strategy by which the film personalises the political is through its use of the romance narrative between Gump and Jenny. Throughout the film this romance organises scenes from the recent American past into the prehistory of a marriage. This marriage triumphantly stands as the sign of the condition of America, unproblematically excluding the civil rights struggles of African Americans, feminists and homosexuals and thereby excluding them from American national identity. That this ideological work is done silently makes it all the more effective.

Notes

1. Rowena Chapman and Jonathan Rutherford, 'The forward march of men halted', in Rowena Chapman and Jonathan Rutherford (eds), *Male Order: Unwrapping Masculinity* (London: Lawrence and Wishart, 1988), pp. 9–18; pp. 11.

2. See Laura Mulvey, *Visual and Other Pleasures* (London: Macmillan, 1989); Richard Dyer, 'White', *Screen* 28/4 (1988), pp. 44–64, and reprinted in Richard Dyer, *The Matter of Images: Essays on Representations* (London and New York: Routledge, 1993), pp. 141–63; a useful and often cited introduction to the ways in which dominant representations of whiteness as blankness underwrite white racial power.

3. Henry A. Giroux, 'Living dangerously: Identity politics and the new cultural racism: Towards a critical pedagogy of representation', *Cultural Studies* 7/1 (1993), pp. 1–27; p. 14.

4. Kaja Silverman, *Male Subjectivity at the Margins* (London and New York: Routledge, 1992).

5. Steven Cohan and Ina Rae Hark (eds), *Screening the Male: Exploring Masculinities in Hollywood Cinema* (London and New York: Routledge, 1993). As their prologue, Cohan and Hark reprint Steve Neale's 1983 *Screen* essay, 'Masculinity as Spectacle', which takes up the interests of Laura Mulvey's work to launch a formal analysis of film representations of masculinity. The bulk of contributions range away from classical film theory, as for example in Chris Holmlund's development of a notion of masquerade used by both sexes 'in order to break down rigid gender-bound dichotomies' (p. 214).

6. Pat Kirkham and Janet Thumim (eds), *You Tarzan: Masculinity, Movies and Men* (Lawrence & Wishart, 1993); *Me Jane: Masculinity, Movies and Women* (Lawrence & Wishart, 1995).

7. Modleski's work is discussed in the Introduction; see also Elizabeth G. Traube, *Dreaming Identities: Class, Gender and Generation in 1980s film* (Boulder and Oxford: Westview Press, 1992).

8. Susan Jeffords, *The Remasculinization of America: Gender and the Vietnam War* (Bloomington and Indianapolis: Indiana University Press, 1989); and *Hard Bodies: Hollywood Masculinity in the Reagan era* (New Brunswick: Rutgers University Press, 1994).

9. In addition to the works cited below, for a combination of culturalist and psycho-analytic approaches to shifting masculinities, see the influential and wide-ranging Lynne Segal, *Slow Motion: Changing Masculinities, Changing Men* (London: Virago, 1990).

10. Admittedly we are extrapolating a little here from the comments in 'The forward march of men halted', quoted above.

11. Susan Jeffords, 'The big switch: Hollywood masculinity in the nineties', in Jim Collins, Hilary Radner, and Ava Preacher Collins (eds) *Film Theory Goes to the Movies* (New York and London: Routledge, 1993), pp. 196–208.

12. Quoted in Jeffords, 'Big switch', pp. 206–7.

13. Fred Pfeil, *White Guys: Studies in Post-modern Domination and Difference* (London: Verso, 1995), p. 49.

14. Traube, *Dreaming Identities*, Chapter 5, 'Who will do the caring? Domestic men and independent women in the movies', pp. 123–69.

15. Traube, *Dreaming Identities*, p. 154.

16. Traube, *Dreaming Identities*, pp. 147–9.

17. Robin Wood, *Hollywood from Vietnam to Reagan* (New York: Columbia University Press, 1986), p. 166.

18. On *Risky Business* see Wood as above and Justin Wyatt, *High Concept: Movies and Marketing in Hollywood* (Austin: University of Texas Press, 1994), pp. 196–8. For a useful discussion of *Ferris Bueller's Day Off* and related comedies in the context of Reaganite ideology, see Traube, *Dreaming Identities*, Chapter 3, 'Secrets of success in post-modern society', pp. 67–96.

19. Pauline Kael, *Fatal Attraction* review in *Cinemania CD-Rom* (Microsoft, 1994).

20. Roger Ebert, *Wall Street* review in *Cinemania*; Traube, *Dreaming Identities*, p. 106.

21. Traube, *Dreaming Identities*, p. 112.

22. Eve Kosofsky Sedgwick, *Between Men: English Literature and Male Homosocial Desire* (New York: Columbia University Press, 1985).

23. See Jude Davies, 'Gender, ethnicity and cultural crisis in *Falling Down* and *Groundhog Day*', *Screen* 36/3 (1995), pp. 214–32; and Jude Davies, ' "I'm the bad guy?" *Falling Down* and white masculinity in 1990s Hollywood', *Journal of Gender Studies* 4/2 (1995), pp. 145–52; pp. 147–8.

24. Joel Schumacher, quoted in Mark Salisbury, 'He's an "ordinary man at war with the everyday world" ', *Empire*, July 1993, pp. 76–8; pp. 77–8.

25. See for example Carol Clover, 'White Noise', *Sight and Sound* (May 1993), pp. 6–9.

26. Werner Sollors, *Beyond Ethnicity: Consent and Descent in American Culture* (New York and Oxford: Oxford University Press, 1986), p. 31.

27. This edition of *Crossfire* exemplifies the consumption of *Falling Down* via news reportage, pitting the liberal Kimmel against Barry Slotnick, the attorney who had successfully defended 'vigilante' Bernard Goetz.

28. Liam Kennedy, 'Alien Nation: White Male Paranoia and Imperial Culture in the United States', *Journal of American Studies* 30/1 (1996), pp. 87–100; p. 96.

29. For further elaboration of this shift see Davies, 'I'm the bad guy?', pp. 149–50.

30. For consideration of some of these significances see the works by Kennedy and Pfeil cited elsewhere.

31. As for example in *Disclosure*, when, accused of sexual harassment, the Douglas character launches into a tirade on the theme of 'When did I have the power?' (see below).

32. Pfeil, *White Guys*, pp. 10–11, 13; see also pp. 239–43 for an insightful reading of *Falling Down* in which he draws attention to what he calls *Falling Down*'s 'Lukácsian work of socio-political typing and assessment'.

33. For further discussion of this point, and the relation of *Falling Down* to political correctness in general, see Davies, 'Gender, ethnicity and cultural crisis', and 'I'm the bad guy?'.

34. Quoted in Wiegman, 'Black bodies', p. 312.

35. On her first appearance, Kaplan explains her presence in Seattle as a visit to her son who is studying at Washington State University; the son appears in the closing scenes of the film to witness his mother's promotion.

36. See for example the work of bell hooks, and Wiegman, 'Black bodies', pp. 310–12.

CHAPTER 2

Transactions in Race and Ethnicity: Positive, Negative and Interrogative Images of African Americans on Film

Power in contemporary society habitually passes itself off as embodied in the normal as opposed to the superior. This is common to all forms of power, but it works in a peculiarly seductive way with whiteness, because of the way it seems rooted, in common-sense thought, in things other than ethnic difference. The very terms we use to describe the major ethnic divide presented by Western society, 'black' and 'white' are imported from and naturalised by other discourses.

Richard Dyer, 'White'[1]

As these media representations of blackness take form, disappear, and reappear, they call up histories, effects, sentiments, and desires. In the process, they seem to generate a certain political urgency for African Americans to interrogate the past critically, locate themelves in the present, and come to terms with their desires for the future. In this moment of struggle over the sign of blackness and terms of a multi-cultural future it is more and more difficult to distinguish progressive political possibilities from neoliberal and conservative rewrites of the same old racial narratives.

Herman Gray, *Watching Race*[2]

The function of race in constructions of American ethnicity

What is at stake in representations of African Americans on film? It might seem that an obvious procedure for this chapter would be to erect a definition of authentic blackness, against which Hollywood images could be judged. Such an approach is not adopted here for the reasons broached in the Introduction and elaborated upon below. With greater misgiving, we have also resisted grounding analysis of cinematic representations by reference to the lived experiences of African Americans, despite the usefulness of such a strategy in enabling the critique and unmasking of demeaning and erroneous representations. While such a procedure also risks fixating on a singular notion of blackness, and might tend to oversimplify practices of consumption such as, for example, via fantasy, recognition and misrecognition, pleasure and displacement, our reasons for foregoing it are largely strategic. By emphasising the nature of racial representations as encoded constructions of identity we aim to throw into relief the interdependence of blackness and other racial and ethnic identities in the production of meaning.

In this frame, 'race' is one category among several modes of identity construction. Nevertheless, as critics from W. E. B. Du Bois to Toni Morrison and Robert Gooding-Williams have shown, constructions of race in general and blackness in particular have been and remain crucial in structuring white-centred American literature and national identity.[3] It is therefore crucial, as Gooding-Williams has argued, that a critique of racial representations does not stop at contesting 'false characterizations', and instead

> should also explore the ways in which explanations and other representations of black bodies function as forms of sociopolitical imagination ... it should investigate the ways in which these representations present themselves as allegories of social organization and political community.[4]

Because Hollywood representations of African Americans have been marked pre-eminently in terms of race and ethnicity, historical accounts of images of race and ethnicity have been couched in terms of the history of the representation of African Americans. Published as recently as 1987, Woll and Miller's historical and bibliographical guide to *Ethnic and Racial Images in American Film and Television* had no listing for Anglo-Americans or white, Anglo-Saxon Protestant representations. Of the ten (plus 'Others') ethnic and racial identities specified, the list is dominated by entries on 'Afro-Americans', which comprise 138 pages out of 312. The historical essay and bibliography on images of Italians, the next most bulky section, comprise only 32 pages. The implications are twofold: first that all of the non-WASP ethnic and racial identities listed qualify in some sense as 'Others', thus inscribing WASP identity as both central and invisible in terms of specific ethnic associations and connotations. Second, the predominance of entries on African Americans implies a hierarchy of otherness, such that historically blackness has been its pre-eminent signifier. Thus we have chosen to examine representations of African American identities not just for their own historical specifics but because they were and continue to be used as an exemplary paradigm for ethnicity in America. We would hope that our reading encourages the examination of other ethnic identities within this paradigm.

Hollywood represents all ethnic identities according to semiotic codes, the most obvious of which are ethnic stereotypes such as the Latin lover, the lazy or lovable Irish. All of these have performed both representative and transactional functions, but blackness has fulfilled a specific function as the pre-eminent signifier of otherness, in defining the norm by what it is not, and thereby as a means of binding together disparate [white] ethnicities into a dominant American identity. As we discussed in Chapter 1, straight white masculinity has long occupied the centred, default position in American culture. Historically, as Cornel West has pointed out, in dominant American culture blackness has functioned to naturalise as American the diversity of ethnicities and nationalities that could be understood at any given historical moment as 'white', i.e. non-black.[5] Thus dominant notions of American ethnic inclusiveness have been predicated on the racial binary. Often the negative charge of blackness functions to secure the positively charged and apparent ethnic inclusiveness of whiteness. As Herman Gray's comments quoted above imply, the significances and transactional uses of ethnic identity have proliferated in the 1980s and 1990s due to the continued use of blackness in this way, alongside such developments as the increased visibility of African Americans on film screens and the demands for and the production of positive images of blacks. In line with Gray, Gooding–Williams and West, this chapter proceeds from the conviction that a concentration on the production of positive images alone is inadequate to deal with the strategic and transactional uses of ethnic identity in American film, uses which have become increasingly complex from the 1980s on.

An early filmic example of the paradigm identified by West is D. W. Griffith's *The Birth of a Nation*. From its release in 1915, it has been the subject of protest and contestation for its negative representations of African Americans. The film's opening in Boston was met with pickets and violent protest, while it also provoked the production of films by African Americans to disseminate positive images of black Americans, as for example the African American film company that named itself *The Birth of a Race*.[6]

The Birth of a Nation has been seen as articulating a biological discourse of racial inferiority, whereby blacks are represented as happiest when dancing or working, and unable to cope with the responsibilities of citizenship. The work of exposing and critiquing these images, and the production and dissemination of positive images of African Americans, is very necessary due to the iconic status of *The Birth of a Nation* in Film Studies and American Studies courses, popularly, and for other filmmakers. At one level, through its representation of the fictional excesses of black-dominated legislatures, the film represents the granting of civil rights to blacks as catastrophic. At another, in bucolic scenes of slaves as plantation workers, black social existence is relegated to myth. In both respects the exclusion of African Americans from political agency and from history can be treated as a matter of negative images. However, an exclusive concentration on contesting negative images does not go far enough in understanding the strategic and transactional uses to which blackness is put in the film, and hence to explain, to unpack and to expose the structures that intersect with and help to reproduce racism. What has historically proved more difficult to contest is the transactional use made of blackness by Griffith, as the means by which whites are united.

The major aim of *The Birth of a Nation* attested to by Griffith was to explain and to justify the Civil War and its context from a truthful and Southern-orientated perspective.[7] The primary ideological project of Griffith's film was the production of a historical narrative of America that would unite white Southerners and white Northerners. Griffith accomplishes this explicitly by interweaving into the representation of historical events such as Civil War battles and Lincoln's signing of the freedom proclamation two romance narratives featuring Northern and Southern whites. The film ends with a marriage which unites the two families whose narratives occupy the bulk of the film: the Camerons of South Carolina and the Stonemans from Pennsylvania; the former plantation owners, the latter, originally, abolitionists. This heterosexual union plays out in romance terms the union between the South and the North and defines both exclusively as white. Covertly, the exclusion and demonisation of blacks, as well as serving to defend the ways of the old South (i.e. slavery), were also a major means by which this work of unifying white identities was achieved. This double use of blackness overlaps with the two modes in which the film represents African Americans. Griffiths uses African American performers in some minor roles, but Gus, the former slave inflamed by carpetbagger rhetoric and lust for a white woman, is played by white actor Walter Long, in blackface.

In this context, the importance of representations of African Americans for Griffith's project lies primarily in establishing, by their otherness, the limits of whiteness as the limits of the American polity. Only secondarily are African Americans represented as such a threat as to require the demonising discourse of biological racism. Thus in a famous scene Gus, a so-called renegade slave, pursues Flora Cameron (played by Mae Marsh, the 'little sister' of the film's nascent Ku Klux Klan activist Ben Cameron) with apparently rapacious intent. She evades him by jumping to her death from a bluff. Extremely offensive as this representation is, its primary function in the narrative is to emphasise the need to reunify Northern and Southern whites rather than to justify and to elicit the racial oppression of blacks. Ultimate responsibility for Gus's behaviour, the film suggests, should be laid at the door of political manipulators, the carpetbaggers and scalawags who have misled him into thinking himself party to the post-war settlement and hence to full citizenship. This does not make the film any less racist, as critics such as William K. Everson have claimed; but rather it articulates racism in more than one way.[8]

Negative, positive and interrogative images

A direct illustration of thinking about the multiple uses of blackness in representative and transactional modes is the work of James Snead collected in *White Screens/Black Images: Hollywood from the Dark Side*.[9] While acknowledging the work of 1970s critics such as Daniel Leab, Donald Bogle and Thomas Cripps, who focused on 'the black image in films', a phrase Snead puts in quotation marks, he calls for thinking about African American identity to go beyond the binary of negative/positive images.[10] 'Such a method,' he argues, 'could not grasp what closer rhetorical and discursive analysis of racial imagery can.'[11] Snead draws on the semiotic theories of Eco and Barthes to demonstrate how Hollywood blackness has functioned in coded terms, signifying a range of things including among others primivitism, the natural, and innocence, almost always as the negative or othered half of a binary opposition such as master/slave, civilised/primitive, enlightened/ backward, good/evil. One of the great strengths of Snead's account is that he combines on the one hand a sense of the multiplicity of codifications associated with blackness with, on the other, an insistence on the power relation within which that multiplicity is inscribed:

> From the very first films, black skin on screen became a complex code for various things, depending on the social self-conception and positioning of the viewer; it could as easily connote white superiority and self-regard as black inferiority ... Onscreen and off, the history that Western culture has made typically denies blacks and black skin of historical reference, except as former slaves or savages.[12]

These insights enable Snead to make detailed and highly perceptive readings of black images in films of classical Hollywood and in black independent films. However, as Colin MacCabe points out in a Foreword to *White Screens/Black Images*, a significant absence from Snead's work, due to his early death, is a consideration of contemporary mainstream pictures featuring African Americans in central roles and spaces.[13] These developments have the potential, arguably, to produce representations of blackness which are subject to different transactional uses, and, still more importantly, are not marginalised but are constructed in ways other than as the negative of a racial binary. At the same time, such films are subject to all the pressures of a crossover cultural form: financial, institutional, and the requirement to be readable by audiences used to Hollywood conventions. Some critics, such as Mark A. Reid and Manthia Diawara, regard these pressures as insuperable and emphasise the recuperative strategies of mainstream Hollywood films against the subversive potential of independent black cinema.[14] Reid begins his *Redefining Black Film* with the assertion that in mainstream film 'a black perspective that acknowledges differences of race, class, gender, and sexuality rarely surfaces', and emphasises the difference between what he terms 'commercial' and 'black independent film production'.[15] However, against the focus of the bulk of the book, Reid's brief comments on crossover filmmakers such as Spike Lee imply that his binary model constructed out of 1960s and 1970s contexts may need some revision in the light of 1990s developments.[16] Therefore we set out here to take up the development implied by MacCabe of a third set of critical positions which go beyond both the negative/positive images debates and the semiotic analyses of blackness.

Like MacCabe, in order to come to terms with, and to effectively expose and contest both the representational and transactional uses of ethnicity and race, most critics tend to identify a three-fold development in the history of racialised images, which is thought of as roughly chronological. The first two stages are generally agreed upon: first the production by Hollywood of negative images, and their contestation and exposure. Second, the production by African Americans and some liberal filmmakers, of 'positive images' which were offered both as correctives to the dominant discourse and as foci of African American identity. Into this category can be placed the so-called 'race films' made by largely black crews for black audiences, many of which were inspired by the reaction against the racial grammar of *The Birth of a Nation*, and the black independent films dating back to the 1920s, and undergoing a resurgence from the late 1960s on. Related to this tradition are examples such as the liberal Hollywood pictures starring Sidney Poitier, the action roles played by black actors such as Danny Glover and Wesley Snipes, and the 1970s 'blaxploitation' films, which tended to be written, produced and directed by whites while featuring black casts, and were double-voiced in terms of their appeal to black and to white audiences.[17]

More recently, critics have identified a third term in this triad, whereby the production of positive images is largely displaced by an attempt to contest the ways in which race and ethnicity as such are represented by Hollywood. First appearing in 1970s independent black films such as Bill Gunn's *Ganja and Hess* (1973), these constructions of African American identity may be termed interrogative images, since they are engaged in contesting not simply the polarity of racial representation, but also the discourses of race and ethnicity – and often also those of gender, class and others; themselves. Theorists have conceptualised these developments in different ways. Here we will discuss two. Manthia Diawara theorises constructions of racial identity not in terms of positive or negative images but in terms of space. Diawara defines the third term in the triad in terms of the aesthetic relation between race and space, and compares the innovative and contestatory production of space in independent black film with what he regards as the continued determination of Hollywood space by a dominant whiteness. Having discussed Diawara's account, we then turn to Cornel West's work on what he calls 'the new cultural politics of difference' to contextualise debates over racial representations on film with respect to the historical development of black diasporic culture. It should be stressed that the identity formation debates which these critics raise are neither separate from a reading of the films nor a revelatory superstructure for their explication, but an integral part of the cultural debate which directors and audiences are clearly aware of.

Manthia Diawara opens his edited collection *Black American Cinema* with a brief discussion of *The Birth of a Nation*, which he views as paradigmatic of Hollywood representations of African Americans, not necessarily for its overt racism but for its initiation of modes of representation whereby blacks are continually marginalised, and shown only in relation to whites. But, on the same page of 'Black American cinema: The new realism', Diawara points out that *The Birth of a Nation* initiated a counter-tradition of films that contested both its overt racism and its marginalisation of blacks.[18] For Diawara, the Hollywood tradition, however overtly liberal, perpetuates the marginalisation of African Americans through its continued representation of blacks in terms of a racial problematic. He therefore emphasises the importance of the black independent tradition in producing contestatory images and representations. Historically, this contestation has been contained in traditions produced and distributed almost exclusively for black audiences, such as the genre known as 'race films', dominated by the films of Oscar Micheaux, and latterly the black independents.

Diawara describes how recent independent African American films have adopted aesthetic strategies which, rather than constituting an alternative tradition, seek to intervene in and to contest the construction of race in Hollywood film. He discerns two aesthetic strands in independent African American film, both of which embody criticisms of Hollywood's racial hierarchy of space in which whites are centralised and blacks marginalised. Diawara connects black cultural production both to notions of modernism and of post-modernism, and refuses to overtly privilege one or the other. He defines the modernist strand as linear, time-based, active, and materially grounded, and embodied in films such as Melvin Van Peebles's *Sweet Sweetback's Baadasssss Song* (1971), *Cooley High* (Michael Schultz, 1975), *House Party* (Reginald Hudlin, 1990), *Chameleon Street* (Wendell B. Harris, Jr., 1991), *Passing*

Through (Larry Clark, 1977), *Do the Right Thing* (Spike Lee, 1989), *Straight Out of Brooklyn* (Matty Rich, 1991), *Juice* (Ernest R. Dickerson, 1992), and *Boyz N the Hood* (John Singleton, 1991). In comparison, Diawara discusses what he calls the post-modernist, space-based, symbolic, reflexive and expressive style of films such as Bill Gunn's *Ganja and Hess* (1973), and *A Powerful Thang* (Zeinabu Davis), *Losing Ground* (Kathleen Collins, 1982), *Killer of Sheep* (Charles Burnett, 1977), *To Sleep with Anger* (Charles Burnett, 1990), *Tongues Untied* (Marlon Riggs, 1989), *She's Gotta Have It* (Spike Lee, 1986), and Julie Dash's *Daughters of the Dust* (1991). He goes on to exemplify the differences in these stylistics, which he argues go so far as to constitute 'different imaginaries derived from the Black experience in America'; the one 'expressive and celebratory', and the other constituting 'existentialist performances of Black people against policing, racism, and genocide'.[19]

As stated, Diawara regards mainstream film and television production as continually dominated by paradigms that marginalise African American identity. He argues that the strategies of positive images and of symbolic representation have failed to challenge the dominant construction of space dominated by white power, and therefore have functioned to keep 'the real contours of the Black community outside Hollywood'.[20] For Diawara, the rare mainstream representations of African American narratives such as the television series *Roots* and Lee's *Do the Right Thing* have only reinforced structures of tokenism and exceptionalism despite what we would regard as the importance of their articulation of a historical or contemporary ethnic identity for a national audience. Diawara therefore looks to the expressive and realist styles of black independent film as modes of producing representations of black histories and of space not dominated by whites, and of contesting white spatial power.

On the face of it, Diawara's explicit privileging of black independent film appears to have little in common with the arguments made in our Introduction. His near absolute distinction between mainstream and independent modes of production seems to negate an interest in crossovers and 'mainstreamisation'. However, there are several indications that his taxonomy is not so rigid as it may at first appear. Unlike that of critics such as Mark A. Reid, Diawara's definition of independent film production includes films that are made independently but distributed by non-black, commercial organisations.[21] Such definitions have been problematised by the role played by small, white-owned independent distribution companies in releasing a large proportion of films by African American directors in the early 1990s. In addition, some contibutors to Diawara's collection, including Richard Dyer, Jacquie Jones, Jacqueline Bobo, and to some extent bell hooks, emphasise the potential for anti-racist and black-centred readings of mainstream film. In fact, having made the distinction between mainstream and independent film, with its materialist overtones, Diawara's real interest lies in the strategic implications of the two modes of film he discusses. Close attention to this argument yields useful strategies for discussing both mainstream and independent black film production.

Diawara fulsomely praises Dash's *Daughters of the Dust*, and he is careful to devote equal space to discussion of the expressive (postmodernist) and the realist (modernist) styles. Although he takes pains to trace the histories of both genres in equivalent detail, and to describe their strategies as securing alternate and complementary ends, without privileging one over the other, nevertheless a sense emerges from the essay, reinforced by its title, that he finds the 'new realism' most exciting and useful. The essay suggests a prioritisation whereby, while the expressive strand of African American independent films serves to construct a black cultural space for inspirational and rejuvenating dialogues with a dynamic black history and culture, it is the realist strand which actively contests dominant white representations of space.

In making a case for the latter, Diawara invokes the notion of a 'rite de passage', a mode appropriated from white culture to frame the difficult entrance into the public world of black youth. The very appropriation of the form highlights the special difficulties attendant on black maturity. Thus at the level of form as well as content, films such as *Boyz N The Hood* call attention to the white dominance of cultural space and set about contesting it. Though for various reasons Diawara does not do so, these formal considerations can be linked with a sense of the marketplace. The overt taking on and contestation of Hollywood conventions about space is more easily readable to mass commercial audiences than is the production of alternative representations of space and identity. Certainly the films listed in the realist category have proved far more attractive to commercial film distributors and are in general far better known and have reached larger audiences than those labelled by Diawara as expressive, with the exception of *Daughters of the Dust*.

Diawara never makes explicit this prioritisation, though some of his terms imply it: he does present the 'new realism' as an 'active' form, which is orientated towards present and future, as compared with the concern with history evinced by the expressive strand. It may be that in part this is due to the compacted issues of gender that surround his categorisation. While none of the films listed as realist were directed by women, three female directors figure as examples of the expressive strand, which is exemplified by a detailed discussion of Julie Dash's *Daughters of the Dust*. Diawara's discussion of his taxonomy bypasses debates over gendered identity and the utility of essentialist versus deconstructive approaches. This is a useful strategy, in that he enables himself to validate both strands, avoiding the necessity of disparaging one to celebrate the other and evading presenting the two strands as fractured halves of an unrestorable whole. However, this does mean that his argument has certain limits. This matters less for Diawara's reading of *Daughters of the Dust*, which is sensitive and persuasive, than for his comments on *Boyz N the Hood*, and his use of the 'rite de passage' model. Diawara does mention one element of the sexism and patriarchalism of the film (in a footnote), but he fails to register the androcentrism of the 'rite de passage' mode, which is historically almost exclusively a genre concerned with young males, whose most obvious recent example from Hollywood is the acutely androcentric *Dead Poets Society*.[22] Diawara comes close to taking for granted the universal applicability of the experiences of young urban black males for all African Americans. This is not to undermine Diawara's categorical distinctions but to regret the omission on his part of explicit consideration of the workings of gender across and within them. Diawara's considerations could well have been forwarded by comparing *Boyz* with a film such as Leslie Harris's *Just Another Girl on the IRT* (1993), which narrates the rites of passage of a doubly marginalised protagonist: a young African American woman's pregnancy and subsequent enrollment in higher education as a single mother. The positive representation by Harris in narrative and cinematic terms of the difficulties of motherhood (her use of the direct address to camera providing, like Lee, an apparently unmediated access to femininity) contrasts with the negative stereotypes employed by Singleton in order to accentuate the importance of models of black masculinity. This makes any straightforward valorisation of such films as *Boyz* problematic. (Released in 1993, the film may have been too late for consideration in Diawara's essay published in the same year.)

Diawara's division of his book into two parts, considering in turn 'Black Aesthetics' and 'Black Spectatorship', allows the discussion of independent and mainstream films alongside one another, but tends to inhibit both enquiry into the construction of blackness, and theorisation of the effects on production and consumption of the penetration of large numbers of black filmmakers and performers into Hollywood in the early 1990s. Diawara's procedure here echoes the flat statement of Clyde Taylor in a 1980s essay, that 'The best approach to black cinema as art is to see it in intimate relation to the full range of Afro-American art expression.'[23] Diawara's book does contain two essays on the work of Spike Lee, though tellingly both are situated in the section on Black Aesthetics, and neither is concerned to theorise Lee in terms of main-streamisation or authenticity.[24] Commercial exigencies also open to question Diawara's discussion of *Daughters of the Dust* and *Boyz N the Hood* as black independent films. Although both were made inde-pendently, they were both picked up for commercial distribution. Whatever the benefits of such an approach, and these are by no means inconsiderable, they risk reinscribing what Cornel West has described as 'the innocent notion of the essential Black subject' or what Henry Louis Gates, Jr. has called the 'transcendent black subject', whereby African American identity is assumed to be present, holistic, and fully realised outside the text.[25]

In his influential 1990 essay 'The new cultural politics of difference', from which the above quotation comes, Cornel West reviews the emphasis on black 'positive' images which was the initial response to and contestation of white supremacist stereotypes in American culture. West finds 'positive images' discourses problematic for several reasons, but principally because they proceed in an 'assimilationist manner' and they rest on a 'homogenizing impulse'. In his view, discourses of positive images are assimilationist because, since these cultural struggles for visibility and respect took place on white-dominated terrain, they could not help but aim to show that black people were 'really like' white people. They are 'homogenizing' because of the assumption that black people were all really alike, which not only negated the impact of other politics (especially of gender, but also of class, age, sexual orientation and so on), but also tended to reproduce the binary oppositional logic of black/white, thereby pre-empting an understanding of how, as West puts it, ' "Whiteness" is a politically constructed category parasitical on "Blackness" '.[26] West therefore celebrates and recommends what he calls a 'new cultural politics of difference' in which black cultural producers utilise new strategies of deconstruction and interrogation:

Black cultural workers must constitute and sustain discursive and institutional networks that deconstruct earlier modern Black strategies for identity-formation, demystify power relations that incorporate class, patriarchal and homophobic biases, and construct more multi-valent and multi-dimensional responses that articulate the complexity and diversity of Black practices in the modern and post-modern world.

Furthermore, Black cultural workers must investigate and interrogate the other of Blackness – Whiteness.[27]

What West's argument offers is the possibility not only of contesting the demeaning effects of white supremacist stereotypes and the marginalisation of black representations but also the transactional uses of images of African Americans. The implication of this passage is that racism has to be understood not simply as a cause but also as an effect, and in this case as fulfilling a strategic function, the securing of alliances among whites of different geographical, cultural, and political affiliations. At the same time and no less importantly, West offers a way of coming to terms with the questioning from within African American culture of androcentric nationalism and of essentialist discourses of identity politics. He forcefully acknowledges the contestatory practices of black women cultural producers, in a manner which throws into relief Diawara's failure to problematise the model whereby black male youth is produced as typical of African American identity.

As well as acknowledging the complexity and diversity of black identity in terms of the internal debates over gender, class, and sexuality, West also looks to a model of black culture which engages with notions of racial hybridity, and which utilises theories and insights from what he calls 'the ambiguous legacy of the Age of Europe'.[28] While West makes very explicit the importance of numerous black diasporic writers, and above all Frantz Fanon, he also alludes in his essay to the European philosophical tradition, to Eurocentric cultural thinkers such as Matthew Arnold and T. S. Eliot, and he mines work by theorists such as Jacques Derrida to provide deconstructive strategies for black cultural production. He thus foregrounds the interrelationship between 'white' and 'black' critical traditions but is less concerned with the resultant modes of production and consumption of a racially hybrid American popular culture.

As we have illustrated, there are sound reasons for West's focusing on the historical development of African American culture, not least in that it helps to redress the marginalisation and minimalisation of black culture. Because of his concentration on the internal dynamics of black culture, considering its relation with European culture only in terms of relation and appropriation, West is not concerned with the complex and ambiguous effects of commerce on the production of (African) American culture. For our purposes, this is particularly important as regards the prominence of black stars from the late 1970s on, such as Richard Pryor, Eddie Murphy, Whoopi Goldberg, Danny Glover, Oprah Winfrey, Bill Cosby, Denzel Washington, Morgan Free-man, Samuel L. Jackson, Whitney Houston, Angela Bassett and Will Smith. This is a comparatively new development in that these African Americans developed star personae, and with it some control over representation both as performers and in some cases directors and pro-ducers. The careers of such performers were driven, partly by individual talent and effort, partly by liberal concerns among some filmmakers, but partly also by the perceived need by Hollywood, in the wake of the 'blaxploitation' films of the early 1970s, to produce films that would appeal to the disproportionately high number (23 per cent) of African Americans who make up the moviegoing public.[29]

This development was itself followed by the coming to prominence of African American directors in studio-distributed pictures. The fore-runner, and regarded by many as the archetype of this, is Spike Lee. Again, this was largely commercially driven, in that black directors appeared, with the ability to bring in low budget films which would earn reasonable box office returns, at a time when Hollywood was concentrating on making fewer, more expensive films, and the number of screens in America was growing.[30] Alongside variegated responses to Lee's films, occasional features on topics such as 'the current state of black film' and its relation to Hollywood appeared in the mainstream press throughout the late 1980s.[31] The breakthrough year is generally regarded as 1991, when in June an article in *Newsweek* proclaimed, 'New Jack Cinema enters screening: With 19 films this year, Hollywood fades to black'.[32] Although this number has not been sustained, and several directors have not repeated the critical and popular success of their first features,[33] the distribution and consumption of these films constitutes a significant development and requires to some extent a rethinking of a rigid binary distinction between black independent films and Holly-wood. In the early 1990s such distinctions were further blurred by the prominence of 'independent' distributors (i.e. independent from Holly-wood studios, though often owned by or with theatre chains, cable and satellite television and other multimedia outlets), and the emergence of new sources of production funding associated with technological shifts in the modes of cinematic distribution, for example, cable and satellite television channels such as HBO, and the development of straight-to-video markets.[34]

West's essay is too early to grapple with the questions posed by this penetration of Hollywood itself by large numbers of African American performers and filmmakers in the late 1980s and early 1990s, and in particular the implications of the circulation of negative, positive, and interrogative images of racial and ethnic identity to mainstream audi-ences. Mainstreamisation is not the only external problematic that needs consideration here. As well as considering the critiques of essentialist forms of identity politics from within African American culture and criticism, it is necessary to appreciate recent shifts in dominant construc-tions of race and ethnicity. The major contexts for the consumption of these 1990s films are threefold: distribution and consumption via more or less mainstream commercial channels; the internal criticisms of ident-ity politics, as described by West and Diawara; and the multiple appropriations of politicised discourses of identity in dominant culture, including mainstream, white-centred, and right-wing modes. The first two of these have been discussed; we now move into our more detailed discussion of exemplary films via a consideration of the third.

'The new racism' and cultural politics in the 1990s

In the late 1980s and early 1990s a variety of critics discerned shifts in the construction of race and ethnicity in dominant American culture. Right-wing white commentators were perceived to have given up a racism based on biological essentialism, and instead appropriated some of the discourses of identity politics. Quoting Pat Buchanan's question 'Who speaks for the Euro-Americans?', Henry A. Giroux identified the following tendency in a 1993 essay:

[R]ight-wing Whites in America now echo a view of difference not as a marker for racial superiority but as a signifier for cultural con-tainment, homogeneity and social and structural inequality. The appeal is no longer to racial supremacy but to cultural uniformity parading under the politics of nationalism and patriotism. In this case, difference is removed from the language of biologism and firmly established as a cultural construct only to be reworked within a hegemonic project that connects race and nation against the elimination of structural and cultural inequality.[35]

Constructions of a 'bad' multiculturalism identified by Giroux here, and articulated by new right ideologues such as Buchanan and Rush Limbaugh, reconstrue and reinforce binaric constructions of ethnic identity such that whites are represented squarely within American traditions of synthesis and assimilation.[36] By contrast non-whites and especially blacks are continually 'othered', at best represented as victims of historical misfortune (cultural), at worst wilfully attached to separatist discourses which privilege their own racial identity (political). Conversely, on the one hand the 'filling in' of white ethnicity ranges between the overtly right-wing demand for a white identity politics (as exemplified by Buchanan's question quoted by Giroux) and a more liberal position whereby, as Giroux puts it, whites become 'self-conscious of race and otherness as central determinants in shaping the existing social, political and cultural landscape ... without having to give up power or privilege.'[37]

Giroux's article is generally downbeat in tone, and he presents the effects of these developments in somewhat monolithic terms via an acerbic reading of *Grand Canyon* (Lawrence Kasdan, 1991). As he shows, *Grand Canyon* makes visible the whiteness of central protagonist Mack (Kevin Kline) as 'a referent for self-sacrifice buttressed by the liberal assumption that as a privileged white man he can solve the problems of marginalised and subordinate Others'.[38] However, consideration of films such as those discussed in the previous chapter shows that the effects of the newly wrought multidimensionality of identity politics are more pluralistic and the power of new racism less absolute than allowed by Giroux here. Not only does a film such as *Falling Down* pluralise the racial typography rendered as a black/white binary in *Grand Canyon*, but its white male central character lacks the economic security from which Mack's power (invisibly) derives. For another thing, unlike in *Grand Canyon*, the right-wing commentators mentioned by Giroux (and again *Falling Down*), for all their power, depend on a logic of crisis which has proved difficult to sustain since it tends to imply a continuing dysfunctionality without ideological focalisation. While successful in rolling back some of the gains made through civil rights legislation they have failed to mobilise permanently a significant proportion of whites. The career of the darling of the new right, Newt Gingrich, suggests the possibility that such politics are electable but lack the ideological framework to realise coherent and workable policies. The failure of Gingrich during his term of office and the poor showing by Pat Buchanan and the more moderate Republican Bob Dole in the 1996 Presidential campaigns has to some extent revealed the new right as, in Raymond Williams's terms, innovating within a declining ideology. As such, it is powerful as a destructive force but remains trapped within a logic of crisis which pre-empts its full elaboration and realisation as a constructive political and ideological programme. Even its futurism is 1950s-style, epitomised by Gingrich's aim to have a personal computer installed in every American home.

It is worth considering that the liberal version of 'new racist' discourse that is in Giroux's view adopted by *Grand Canyon* coexists in the film with more traditional symbolic appeals to ethnic inclusiveness. The film traces the development of a friendship between immigration lawyer Mack (Kevin Kline) and Simon (Danny Glover), a mechanic who saves Mack from being assaulted by a black gang when his Lexus car breaks down. The film is literally grounded by its closing scene, in which Simon drives his sister and nephew, with Mack and family, to the Grand Canyon. As Giroux puts it

> It is here in the face of the wonder of nature that the immensity of the racial, cultural, political, economic and social differences that separate these families are erased in a New Age notion of unity and spirituality.[39]

In this case, although Giroux does not spell out the connection, New Age notions come to constitute a barely updated erasive transcendentalism, in which the landscape of the Grand Canyon is itself the means by which is produced the semblance of unity and equality among blacks and whites. It is of course a commonplace of critical American Studies that such appeals rest on the erasure of history (in this case racial difference, inequality and oppression) by the extra-social figure of the landscape as symbolic of American identity and nationhood.

The case of *Grand Canyon* also focuses debates over positive/negative images, especially concerning the Danny Glover character Simon, who is described by K. Anthony Appiah as fulfilling a comparatively newly created African American stereotype which he terms the 'Saint', or the 'ethical principle' of the movie.[40] While the 'Saint' seems to be related to the historical stereotype of the Tom, Appiah argues that the recent developments of a black star system and the results of campaigns for positive images such as the NAACP's 'image awards' make it an ambiguous figure. For Appiah, this ambiguity is constituted by, among other considerations, rival readings of Simon as a 'positive image', and hence a victory for lobbying such as that of the NAACP; or via a Christian notion of the ennobling effects of suffering, recalling some versions of Martin Luther King's politics but played here as a means of assuaging white guilt and reassuring white audiences (a reading which Giroux might find substantially convincing).[41] Appiah goes on to route this ambiguity through an argument for the importance of consumers in the production of cultural meaning, as against the sometimes static systems invoked in critical interventions. These are timely considerations, but need not and, we would argue, should not obviate placing these ambiguities in the context of considerations of the usefulness of discourses of positive images, and a sense of the transactional nature of the 'Saint' role in its function to reassure white viewers. The question of the politics of a film's representations of identity is an explicit concern for many viewers, including not least those whose consumption of movies is explicitly or implicitly mediated through notions of racist or sexist representation. Care must be exercised here: as Appiah warns us, consumers are able to re-read subversively and to appropriate images that might be positioned by analysis in dominant and white-centred structures of meaning. However, any final conclusions regarding the cultural politics of *Grand Canyon* must include consideration of the tensioned relationship between Danny Glover's star status and filmic persona, and the significance of his performance both as 'positive image' and in transactional terms. Even so, *Grand Canyon* illustrates the continued white dominance over most Hollywood constructions of space.

Appiah is right to stress the overdetermined nature of the 'Saint' stereotype as being situated at the juncture of campaigns for positive images, the need to exorcise white liberal guilt, and the development of African American stars in Hollywood. However, Glover's power as a draw (an index of his star status) must work against the transactional uses of the 'Saint' stereotype, here defined principally by the need to reassure white audiences. In any case, it is clear that a consideration of the transactional uses of such representations of identity must supplement straightforward considerations of positive and negative images.

What this might mean in terms of critical perspectives can be illustrated by a very brief discussion of *Ghost* (Jerry Zucker, 1990), a film which gives Appiah momentary pause since Whoopi Goldberg plays a petty con woman (though he is quick to point out her saintly qualities).[42] *Ghost* is also mentioned in passing by Robert Gooding-Williams, in an essay which seeks to utilise James Snead's 'rhetorical and discursive analysis of racial imagery'.[43] In 'Black cupids, white desires: Reading the recoding of racial difference in *Casablanca*', Gooding-Williams questions the basis on which earlier writers on black Hollywood had validated the representation of the pianist Sam (played by Dooley Wilson) as a positive image of African American dignity.[44] Gooding-Williams argues that the primary narrative function of the Sam role in Michael Curtiz's 1942 classic is that of 'mythical Cupid', facilitating the love affair between the white male and white female protagonists Rick and Ilsa.[45] Racial difference is thus encoded in terms of the functionality of the African American in a narrative of white heterosexuality. Thus for Gooding-Williams a straightforward concern with positive/negative images must be supplemented with attention to the transactional uses to which constructions of identity are put. We would go further, in arguing that the development of African American stars in Hollywood further complicates these representations.

In an aside, Gooding-Williams lists several other films in which 'black cupids' appear, among them *Ghost*, where Whoopi Goldberg mediates between the dead Patrick Swayze character and his wife (Demi Moore). There is much about *Ghost* that supports Gooding-Williams's positioning of the film alongside *Casablanca*. However, unlike Wilson, by 1990 in *Ghost* Goldberg possessed a strong screen persona which was primarily constructed out of Hollywood versions of race and gender politics (principally in *The Color Purple*, Steven Spielberg, 1985). Moreover, this persona was articulated in *Ghost* to explicitly contest, and to partially resist the supplementarity of the black cupid's narrative function. As amateur spiritualist Oda Mae Brown, Goldberg initially protests mightily against her use as mediator by the Swayze and Moore characters. Though this is usually turned to comic effect, even the comedy emphasises tension between Goldberg/Brown's autonomy and her mediating role in the romantic narrative of her co-stars. Unlike Wilson too, Goldberg's performance was rewarded with an Oscar, for best actress in a supporting role. To some extent these differences are accounted for by accidentals. Goldberg was already an established name, though she had not matched the success of *The Color Purple* five years earlier, while *Casablanca* was only Wilson's second film, appearing in the same year as his debut. It is also possible to read Goldberg's performance through the stereotype of the 'sassy' African American female. However, it should be clear that the echoing presence of politicised notions of identity in Goldberg's persona does make a difference to the consumption of the movie.

Giroux, like many culturalist critics, calls for a revivified understanding of identity contextualised with respect to histories, responsibilities and power relations, consciousness of all of which is evacuated by right-wing appropriations of the discourses of identity politics such as Buchanan's appeal to a privatised ethnic identity as the fount of political authority. Concerns about and attempts to work through essentialist modes of gender and racial identification predate the 'new racism' identified by Giroux, and can be found most markedly in the work of African American feminists and womanists such as Audre Lorde, Toni Morrison, and bell hooks, as West acknowledged.[46] Nevertheless, the emergence of the 'new racism' has intensified the perceived need to contest racial essentialism and androcentric nationalism within academic and popular writing. Further impetus has come from the persistence of racial essentialism and androcentric nationalism in black popular culture (most obviously rap culture as well as film), which itself requires critical understanding.[47]

It is apparent that in certain social locations, essentialist and androcentric constructions of African American identity can function to have locally and unevenly empowering effects. Goldberg's portrayal of a separatist African American mother (Sarah Mathews) and bookstore owner in the comedy *Made in America* (Richard Benjamin, 1993) illustrates this. The film mediates the racial problematics of paternity and ethnicity by intercutting the narrative of her daughter's search for her sperm donor father, initially discovered to be the white Hal Jackson (Ted Danson), with a romance between Goldberg and Danson. The film's representation of this romance is clearly hesitant in showing any sexual element and plays it instead largely for comedic effect. The narrative is resolved as Danson is not the father, thus securing black essentialism. Nevertheless, the Goldberg and Danson characters will continue the relationship, therefore including a white audience. To call

for the deconstruction of these images may not necessarily yield immediately liberating results, especially in the context of a 'new racism'
which denies or seeks to ignore the historical determinations of race.

The rest of this chapter will therefore concentrate on various constructions of African American identity in 1990s films. A major focus
will be on two films starring Denzel Washington. This allows us to take
account of developments such as the growth of African American stars
in Hollywood, to discuss work by two directors, one Jewish and one
African American, and enables implicit comparison with the performances of Michael Douglas as discussed in Chapter 1. Both Washington
and Douglas play roles that engage explicitly and implicitly with
politicised notions of identity. Because most of Washington's films
depend on Hollywood finance and structures for production as well as
distribution, and in order to focus issues of representations of African
American women in independently produced film we will also review
the constructions of identity in Julie Dash's *Daughters of the Dust*. Such
independent productions counter the generic containment in comedy
that the case of Goldberg illustrates.

Our focus is therefore not on the male-directed urban films most
famously associated with African American cinema in the 1980s and
1990s. Like Lubiano, Michele Wallace has criticised the work of filmmakers such as Singleton and Lee as conservative, unreflectingly
essentialist and dehistoricising through a reading of their representations
of black masculinity.[48] Their choice of locations in contemporary urban
space, dislocated from either the history of slavery or the migration
north and the effect these contexts had on the formation of black identity,
results in a representation of black masculinity whose power and stability
tends to be shown through the negative othering of black femininity.
While one response to this would be a valorisation of alternative feminist
representations such as Harris, as bell hooks has warned in a discussion
of the similarly misogynist genre of rap music, to either replace or
suppress such representations is to miss the point. They must instead be
understood in their larger social and historical frame:

> The sexist, misogynist, patriarchal ways of thinking and behaving
> that are glorified in gangsta rap are a reflection of the prevailing
> values in our society, values created and sustained by white supre-
> macist capitalist patriarchy.[49]

Hooks contrasts rap music with a reading of *The Piano* (Jane Campion,

New Zealand, 1993) where she maintains a similar misogyny operates. While hooks's reading of rap is acute, her critique of *The Piano* does not recognise the reworking of the genre and romance narrative in a manner which historicises and counters the prevailing patriarchy. In fact we would argue that the history or period film is central to the understanding of contemporary ethnic identities since such films can articulate and contextualise narratives of oppression, while furthering efforts to reinvigorate the projects that began in terms of identity politics.

Glory (Edward Zwick, 1989), *Daughters of the Dust*, and *Malcolm X* are historical films, which portray their subject matter through a sense of recent debates over race, identity and representation. As such they further the recovering or rewriting of histories previously marginalised or erased, a tradition associated with the self-consciousness of racial and gendered identity that developed in the 1960s. But they also do more than this. They are all concerned to produce corrective representations of African Americans which both engage with contemporary debates over racial identity and contest the effects of the white dominance of Hollywood. *Glory*, which represents the black soldiers who fought in the Civil War, attempts to explode Hollywood stereotypes of black masculinity, and goes some way to defamiliarising the white-centredness dominant in Hollywood. The independently funded *Daughters of the Dust* breaks more fundamentally with dominant Hollywood constructions of space and race. It focuses primarily on the female members of an extended black family in the Gullah or Sea Islands off the Georgia coast at the turn of the century. *Daughters of the Dust* was in fact the first feature-length film directed by an African American woman to be given national theatrical release, on which it proved widely popular, demonstrating the existence of a market for films which do not reproduce Hollywood film grammar and conventions. Like *Glory*, Spike Lee's *Malcolm X* routes concerns with representations of positive images and interventions in constructing history through a concern with the iconicity of black masculinity.

Glory: African American history as male rites of passage

Glory tells the story of the 54th Massachusetts Volunteer Infantry, one of the first black regiments ever raised in the USA, from their organisation in the winter of 1862–3 to their leadership of the assault on Fort

Wagner outside Charleston on 18 July 1863. This assault, as the closing scenes of the film portray, was unsuccessful, but the bravery of the African American soldiers of the 54th Massachusetts, who had suffered 50 per cent casualties, became well known. *Glory* can be regarded as an attempt to exorcise the influence of *The Birth of a Nation*. It embarks on a double project of accurately depicting a historical narrative and of problematising and correcting Hollywood representations of the Civil War in particular and African Americans in general. The issues of identity and representation that we have discussed above ensure that there is some tension between these aims. The privileging of historical accuracy implies the use of cinematic conventions in a naturalised way, so that audiences consume the film as a direct representation of history. This would imply that the film utilise a straightforward Hollywood realism. However, the problematisation of discourses of positive images, and the attention given to the ways in which dominant Hollywood conventions racialise space according to white domination, suggest that the film must go some way to undermine and even to defamiliarise the conventions of Hollywood realism in order to contest racist representations.

The scenario of African Americans being integrated into the fighting forces of the Union, which remained racist in culture and practice, crystallises this tension. It would have been possible to represent this narrative via the stories of prominent African Americans who played leading roles in the development and leadership of the 54th Massachusetts, such as Frederick Douglass and his sons. Such a narrative might fit reasonably smoothly into dominant Hollywood conventions which privilege a few heroic figures who function as active agents with important narratives. Interestingly, this is exactly the form taken by the documentary which accompanied the video release of the film, which is entirely concerned with the experiences of African Americans, and includes footage not used in the final cut of *Glory* which focuses directly on Frederick Douglass.[50] Yet this kind of integrationist narrative tends to ground a multiculturalist reading of American history in what Ella Shohat and Robert Stam have called, in a different context, 'a narrowly national and exceptionalist grid, as when well-meaning curriculum committees call for courses about the "contributions" of the world's diverse cultures to the "development of *American* society".'[51]

Instead of concentrating exclusively on black experiences *Glory* reconstructs the story of the 54th Massachusetts through the interwoven narratives of six main characters: the whites Col. Robert Gould Shaw (Matthew Broderick) and his second-in-command Cabot Forbes (Cary Elwes), and four black soldiers. The latter are carefully differentiated in terms of class, position and character, to such an extent that their representation is typological, as will shortly be discussed. They are the young escaped slave Trip (Denzel Washington, given second billing to Broderick), the fatherly onetime grave-digger Sgt. Rawlins (Morgan Freeman), the youthful, stuttering Sharts (Jihmi Kennedy), and Andre Braugher as Searles, well-educated (he quotes Emerson), and a boyhood friend of Shaw. The central figure is Robert Shaw. He is the only one of the principal characters who is not fictional, and the film uses passages from his letters, a fact announced in the opening titles to vouch for its historical authenticity.

The use of a white character to provide the central consciousness through which the film's narratives are mediated provoked some adverse comment, as for example in Roger Ebert's review available on the *Cinemania* CD-ROM, and has probably contributed to the film's failure to attract much critical attention in the context of black film. However, the film does incorporate two major strategies for problematising both the position of Shaw as a white viewer, and the white dominance of Hollywood space in general. A less radical strategy consists of a series of recognition and defamiliarisation scenes, when protagonists Shaw, Forbes and Trip are forced separately to confront their racial mis-perceptions and prejudices. By far the most numerous and striking of these scenes feature the whites Shaw and Cabot, who are shaken out of patronising attitudes and lack of belief in the capacities of the black soldiers, in order to inspire them both to fight for proper resources, and to demand hard standards of training which will enable the black recruits to reach battle readiness. These may be read as providing an object lesson for white audience members. Significantly also, but with much less screen time and far fewer point-of-view shots, Trip is made to confront his conviction that all whites are the same. In spite of the film's paralleling of these shifts in perception across racial lines, its primary focus on the narrative and the perspectives of a white commander cannot help but decentre African American history in a film which purports to be uncovering it.

Yet there are signs that the film is intended to engage with race, history, and representation in more complex ways than the direct telling of historic 'truths' or the production of 'positive images'. While Shaw's

narrative dominates, and his perspective is centralised, the film problem-
atises the normativeness of the white gaze associated with him,
representing his perceptions as limited and subject to error *because of
his racial position*. As the central protagonist of *Glory*, Shaw is associated
with the dominant white male gaze normalised by Hollywood. But many
times in the film, instead of being represented as ostensibly universal
and reliable, this white male gaze is shown to be racially inflected, limited
and subject to misperception. In addition to this, the film undermines
another set of Hollywood conventions; stereotypes of African American
masculinity. These constitute a more cinematically radical set of
strategies than the film's direct representation of Shaw's rite of passage
as a change in his perceptions of African Americans.

The representations of the black soldiers relate to two sets of Hollywood stereotypes. The headstrong youth (Trip), the father-figure
(Rawlins), the backwoods recruit (Sharts), and the bookish, middle-class
recruit (Searles) are derived from classic war movies. In *Glory* these are
brought up against Hollywood stereotypes of African American masculinity. Private Trip's talk patterns, his youth and his highly developed
physique flirt with the Hollywood stereotype of the buck, an identification made explicit by both the racist Irish Sergeant, Mulcahy, and, in
very different tones, among an exclusively black male group, by
Rawlins. After Trip is found outside the camp, Shaw also reads Trip in
this manner, and has him whipped for desertion. Later, it is made clear
that this is a misrecognition when Rawlins explains that Trip had left
the regiment in search of shoes. What Trip does do in black and in
mixed race company is to assert verbally the existence of the power
relation between whites and blacks. In the context of the army, this
amounts also to an insistence on the persistence of racial difference
against the integration along patriachal lines that Shaw is attempting to
achieve. Thus, for example, after Sgt. Mulcahy, having humiliated
Searles during bayonet training, offers the reconciliatory 'Ain't no
shame, son', Trip intervenes with an insistence on racial difference,
'Nigger jus' forgot to duck; that's all.' At one level, then, the 'buck'
stereotype is demonstrated to constitute a misperception in the minds
of the white protagonists. At another, it is associated with a separatist
politics. During the film Trip undergoes a rite of passage in which he
loses the racial chip on his shoulder, and gradually finds common ground
with white commanders. Some trust is established in a one-to-one scene
with Shaw directly before the climactic assault, though Trip continues

to insist 'I still ain't gonna carry your flag'. Much more powerfully, in the battle scenes he takes up the Stars and Stripes after Shaw is killed. Thus in his dying moments, Trip symbolically becomes fully American.

As the father-figure who mediates between whites and blacks, Sgt. Major Rawlins (Morgan Freeman) recalls that of the Tom stereotype. He encounters Shaw in the film's opening scenes, as a grave-digger on the battleground on which Shaw is slightly wounded. Due to his age, Rawlins is the sole one of the central protagonists not to go through a rite of passage within the film's narrative. At the other extreme is the youthful Southerner Sharts, whose rite of passage is quite directly to grow up. It is he who breathlessly intones after the exigencies of training that 'We men now.'

Searles (Andre Braugher) is what Private Trip, echoing a distinction made by Malcolm X, calls a 'house nigger'. His education, his physical appearance (he wears glasses, the sure Hollywood sign of a weakling, an intellectual, or both) and his middle-class affiliations mark him out from the rest of the soldiers. His rite of passage involves the very painful giving up of his personal closeness with Shaw, in order to conform to military discipline. The film represents this trajectory in terms of the development of personal independence.

The treatment of stereotypes and the rites of passage motif are used in *Glory* in ways which imply a rethinking of notions of positive images. As discussed above, Cornel West has identified two problematic elements of traditional discourses of positive images; the 'assimilationist manner' and the 'homogenizing impulse'. Although West's essay delimits its subject as African American cultural production, such tendencies can often be found in images produced by white liberals (Zwick is Jewish). It is possible that the story of African American recruits to the Union Army might reproduce these logics, but *Glory* decisively breaks with them. In terms of racial differentiation, the film pluralises black masculinity into the variety of types just described. Whiteness is binarised into the racially hostile (openly racist senior officers, including the quartermaster who initially refuses to provide the 54th with shoes), and the sympathetic but patronising (including Shaw and Forbes in the early part of the film). The film emphasises that the assault on Fort Wagner was a military failure and that the Fort was never taken during the Civil War. The central struggle that structures *Glory*, represented in the film with the most vivid antagonisms, is not against the Confederacy, but against racial prejudice within the Northern forces, and the white Northerners themselves. The heroic trajectory of the black soldiers then is not constructed according to traditional notions of war heroism, but is played out in terms of rites of passage whose narratives are constructed explicitly in terms of racial sameness and difference.

Moreover, Shaw and Forbes, the white leaders of the 54th, also undergo their own rites of passage during the film which prevents them standing as static models of whiteness to which the African American characters may aspire. Both must lose their patronising sympathy for blacks, while Shaw especially is shown as having to deal also with his shyness and his fear of battle. In early scenes Shaw is established as lacking the bravery of the conventionally good soldier. Intensely anxious under fire, he succumbs to a minor wound at the battle of Antietam Creek. His injury, a piece of dialogue informs us, does not even need the attentions of a surgeon, and its treatment is pointedly accompanied by the agonised screams of a soldier having his leg sawn off. A few minutes later, while Shaw is recuperating at home, the camera dwells on a soldier in a wheelchair. Slightly shellshocked but growing in determination, Shaw is not the traditional commander, but, in keeping with the film's liberal positioning, he is a war hero acutely conscious of the horrors of war.

Significantly, the presentation of white and black soldiers in this way breaks with historical accuracy. The real Shaw was a much more powerful figure and there is little evidence in his letters of the self-doubt attributed to him in the film. Still more importantly, in purely historical terms the film misrepresents the nature of the black soldiers recruited to the 54th. The film represents them as mostly from the South, ex-slaves, and generally illiterate. On the contrary, the African Americans who volunteered for the regiment were mostly from the North, had been born free, were educated, and therefore left a historical record of their experiences in diaries and letters. This material is not used at all in *Glory* but features strongly in *The True Story of Glory Continues*, the documentary made to accompany the film's video release. The recruits included members of prominent black families, and in fact one of Frederick Douglass's sons was sergeant major of the regiment. One implication of this is that the history of the African Americans in the 54th was well known during the war and in the immediate post-war period. It was not lost due to lack of evidence, but erased by powerful myths of white solidarity like *The Birth of a Nation*. In falsifying their identities, Zwick and screenwriter Kevin Jarre did make the men of the 54th more typical of the African Americans in service in the Civil War.[52] But we would suggest more strategic reasons for the change which privilege a project of contesting representations rather than filling in a historical gap. Instead of giving audiences what might be perceived by some as 'positive images' of educated, integrated middle-class blacks taking up arms against the South, what *Glory* shows is a series of rites of passage in which coming to manhood is a matter of self-revelation and military discipline. This structuring narrative of the film's representation of African Americans is summarised by Rawlins (Freeman) who stoops to explain to a group of Southern black children gaping at the African Americans in uniform. 'That's right', he says ' – ain't no dream. We run away slaves and we come back fighting men.' High among the pleasures offered to both black-identified and white-identified audiences is that of observing the transformation represented in the film as from slavery to manhood.

In spite of these considerations, the prominence of Shaw in *Glory* tends to decentre the history and the experiences of African Americans even in a film which is directly concerned with restoring their historical prominence. Almost every scene features Shaw either as protagonist or as viewer. Rather than using the conventions of Hollywood realism to align audiences with the points of view of the black soldiers, *Glory* adopts the more ambitious, and perhaps more risky strategy of centring on Shaw's point of view, while demonstrating its limitations in a variety of ways. We have already pointed to his relationship with Trip, where Shaw's perceptions are shown to be fallible, according to realist conventions. Again, in several scenes the black soldiers are shown marching barefoot, while it takes Trip's example and Rawlins's explanation before Shaw realises the problem. Such examples might loosely be racialised; more striking in racial terms is the film's depiction of the distribution of arms among the soldiers. A white male figure hovers in the background while Rawlins gives out rifles. Then the film cuts to shots of soldiers play-acting with the firearms, and cuts again to Shaw looking on anxiously. Audiences may read the immediately preceding scenes in a variety of ways which might be more or less inflected by racial identification: Hollywood stereotype (blacks with guns are dangerous) or white fear. Whatever these reactions, the cut to Shaw's worried-looking face draws audience attention to the prominence of his perspective.

What is at stake here is the explicit identification of the taken-for-granted, supposedly universal and neutral gaze of Hollywood convention with a privileged, and racially white position. This is enacted in subtle ways in many parts of the film, and is especially overt when passages from Shaw's letters are used in voice-over. The film's opening title, before even the production company logo sequence, introduces Shaw and announces that his letters are collected 'in the Houghton Library of Harvard University'. Seconds later, a panorama of exclusively white Union soldiers are shown cooking, receiving letters, playing baseball, preparing for battle, and Matthew Broderick's voice begins, 'Dear Mother ...'. There is consistency here between view and voice-over. What the audience hears is the voice both of a participant in and a relaxed observer of the human (actually exclusively white and male) pageant they are viewing. A little over half an hour later, the film offers a parallel scene of the newly enlisted African American recruits at ease, again accompanied by Broderick's voice-over reading what purports to be one of Shaw's letters. On this occasion, however, his point of view is ironised by what the audience sees. Broderick's voice describes the soldiers in terms of emulating white soldiers and in terms of racial difference:

Dear Mother, the men learn very quickly, faster than the white troops it seems to me ... the moment they are released from drill, every tongue is relaxed and every ivory tooth is visible and you would not know from the sound of it that this is an army camp ...

What the audience actually sees are soundless images of African American men engaged in such activities as petting a goat, reclining, sitting contemplatively, practising drill among themselves, teaching and learning to read (Searles and Sharts), shaving the head (Trip), and, for a few moments only, a couple of soldiers moving their lips in what looks like singing. Such discontinuities problematise Shaw's assumption of the dominant gaze. At the same time, they undermine any sense that the black soldiers' trajectory in the film is one of racial emulation and assimilation.

The scene is one of several that invoke and expose the ways in which Hollywood conventions (voice-over, point of view, camera work) have been organised along lines of white dominance. Often in *Glory* the cinematic gaze is particularised in terms of white power, and shown to have only limited perceptual accuracy. Perhaps the most striking of these takes place during the army's stay at Beaufort, South Carolina. The film cuts to a tight shot of rows of black children singing 'My

Country 'Tis of Thee'. As they sing, the camera pulls back to reveal the exclusively white audience, dressed in military uniforms and the dresses of Southern belles, for whom the children are performing. The invocation of *Gone with the Wind* serves to heighten the awkwardness of the scene and to point to the conventionality of Hollywood's production of white dominance of space. Another scene completely superfluous to the narrative makes a coded reference to racist Hollywood stereotypes of African Americans. It shows Shaw galloping a horse through a path lined by stakes, each of which has a watermelon stuck on top, slashing at each one with his sword.[53]

The film's cutting and editing foregrounds the power and the meaning of looking, from the black soldiers' keenness to get into uniform to the variety of looks elicited by them marching in uniform, from white civilians, white soldiers and blacks. The first public parade of the regiment is shot to emphasise a series of returned glances. Marching down Main Street at the head of his troops, Shaw makes eye contact with a group of dignitaries including Frederick Douglass, and then on a separate balcony his family. The camera then picks up Trip and Searles catching the eye of the Irish Sergeant Mulcahy, who is in the crowd, while Trip alone meets the gaze of the dignitaries. Searles, Sharts and Rawlins exchange glances with a variety of African Americans in the crowd, whose expressions range from proud to anxious. Still more striking, when the regiment travels south, are the looks of the black children who see African Americans in uniform for the first time. In these scenes, as with the episodes set in the tent shared by Trip, Rawlins, Sharts and Searles, the perspective of any protagonist is not much privileged over the others. When the centrality of Shaw's gaze is to an extent displaced, no authoritative position is supplied by the film's protagonists, but neither is the audience offered an easy voyeurism.

While the construction of visual images in *Glory* foregrounds issues of racialised space and power, its dialogue overtly references debates over racial identity. Some of the relevant passages have been quoted already, since the dialogue plays a major structuring role in defining identity. A major function of the words spoken in *Glory* is to construct the transformation being undergone by the men of the 54th as from slaves, or 'niggers', to 'men'. The rite of passage into manhood is used to invoke the military as an exclusively male family, which offers a structure of relation in which racial difference can be negated. It is hard to convey the number of times the notion of a standardising masculinity is invoked in the film to transcend racial difference. Shaw discusses his men in the voice-overed letters and argues with Forbes over their development, while we have already mentioned its articulation by Rawlins and Sharts.

The limit case for the appeal to this discourse of transcendent masculinity is the Irish Sergeant Mulcahy, a strict and overtly racist sergeant major brought in by Shaw to instil military discipline. The bewildering range of jibes Mulcahy uses on the troops include 'bloody Hindus', and 'ugly Mexican African fuckin whores'. Trip and Searles come in for special abuse. The former is addressed as 'you half-wit black bastard; is it true they cut your balls off at birth? I'm gonna work on you you bastard 'till I get you ... broken'. Mulcahy calls Searles 'a prissy little schoolgirl', 'Bonnie Prince Charlie' and asks with high sarcasm, 'Are you a Senator ... or are you the bloody President of Africa?' Mulcahy invokes notions of growing up and making men to defend his harsh regime, asking Shaw to let his boyhood friend Searles 'grow up some more'. The Irishman makes an uneasy figure in the film. His racist language is alienating, yet he plays a crucial role in the rites of passage of the black soldiers. What holds these together is the invocation of manhood as a transcendent masculinity whose achievement negates the racial, ethnic, and gendered slurs made by Mulcahy. Trip alone remains hostile to this patriarchal discourse of masculinity which offers to transcend racial specificity.

Shortly after the training period, Trip challenges Searles's aspirations to something he identifies as whiteness. Trip explicitly rejects the possibility of emulating white soldiers, telling Searles with heavy sarcasm,

Yeah. Button up that collar, suck in that gut, tuck in them big black lips, lighten your skin, shrink up that nose ... Let me tell you something boy. You can march like the white man, you can talk like him, you can, you can learn his song, you can even wear his suits, but you ain't never gonna be nothing to him but an ugly-assed chimp in a blue suit.

Trip goes on to make noises like a chimp to provoke Searles into a fight. Breaking up the argument, Rawlins fiercely rejects Trip's diatribe in the name of a common masculinity, 'We have to be MEN,' and rejects also Trip's use of the word 'nigger'. He goes on 'You watch who you calling nigger. 'F any niggers round here its you. Smart mouth, stupid-ass, swamp-running nigger. 'F you ain't careful that's all you gonna be.' After this stinging rebuke is delivered, the camera lingers on Trip's face for several seconds.

Obviously a direct reading of this scene would regard Trip's assertion of absolute racial difference as having been invoked only to be disavowed, with the long take on Washington's face as evidence of inner change on the part of Trip whereby his fierce anti-white sentiments are being mellowed. However, the film's continual evocation of racism among Northern whites, the incisiveness of Trip's comments and the power and flamboyance of Washington's performance all work to produce him as a possible separatist icon. Tellingly, for example, at one point he reminds Shaw that when the war is over, Shaw will take up again his middle-class, privileged position, in stark contrast to the African Americans under his command.

In the film's narrative Shaw will not return to his big family house in Boston at the end of the war as Trip has suggested; instead, he dies in battle. It is possible to read the whiteness produced for Shaw in *Glory* like that of Mack in *Grand Canyon*, in the terms described by Henry Giroux, discussed earlier; that is as 'a referent for self-sacrifice buttressed by the liberal assumption that as a privileged white man he can solve the problems of marginalised and subordinate Others'.[54] Perhaps many (white) viewers did so. However, this is not only to smooth over the formal discontinuities associated with Shaw's point of view in the film, but to dismiss entirely the insistent voicing of racial difference by Trip. That Washington's performance obtained the film's only acting Oscar (for best actor in a supporting role) implies that its force was often recognised. Ultimately these readings pivot on the film's final scenes, set in battle and its aftermath, where dialogue is dispensed with and image is dominant. The two dominant images are Trip's taking up of the Stars and Stripes banner after Shaw falls, and the last frames, which show first Shaw's and then Trip's body being tipped into an open grave. The two bodies come to rest in a position of intimacy which might symbolise an accommodation impossible while both men were alive. The question is whether Trip has had to renounce his politicised sense of racialised identity in order to find common cause with the white-led Northern Army. In refusing to explicitly settle this question, the film may be considered evasive. It might also be read as refusing reductivist notions of either integration or separatism. Instead, political relations between African Americans and white Americans are constructed as subject to continual negotiation.

Nevertheless, the constructions of racial identity in *Glory* remain problematic on two counts. The use of a version, even reworked and ironised, of the 'buck' stereotype to represent the separatist position implies a major limitation to its self-consciousness about Hollywood stereotypes. *Glory* might have been a different film again if the filmmakers had been able to imagine the educated Searles, or the fatherly Rawlins, voicing separatist sentiments, having a double consciousness, or even as ever wavering in their affiliation with Northern white authority. Strangely enough, *The True Story of Glory Continues* documentary contains some scenes shot for the film which addressed comparable aspects of debate among African Americans over participation in the war, including a hotly contested debate at a recruitment meeting. However, along with other material featuring Frederick Douglass, these did not make the final cut. Still more strikingly, it is clear that *Glory* achieves its troubled negotiation of black/white relationships by construing racial relations in exclusively male terms.

Tensioned and interlocking identities in *Daughters of the Dust*

Daughters of the Dust has been celebrated by many critics for its innovative constructions of race and space.[55] While we have treated *Glory* as in some limited ways subverting the white-dominated film grammar of Hollywood, Julie Dash's film has been regarded as forging different modes of representation appropriate to histories of people of African descent in America, and of African American female identity in particular. Allied with this project *Daughters of the Dust* aspires to a more democratic kind of cinema which refuses to fetishise one or two central heroic protagonists. Dash's use of dual narration, multiple points of view, non-linear and layered unfolding, and cinematographer Arthur Jafa (AJ)'s utilisation of techniques such as wide depth of field, non-standard lighting, and shifting film speed, have all been remarked upon as marking *Daughters of the Dust* out from Hollywood conventions. Since these have been ably described by Toni Cade Bambara, Ed Guerrero, and by Manthia Diawara in the piece discussed above, we will not be primarily concerned here with these innovations. Instead, we will concentrate on some related achievements of the film: its sustaining of multiple tensioned and antagonistic discourses of identity.

In an interview with bell hooks published in the book *Daughters of the Dust*, Dash stated that her priority in making the film was to address first black women, the black community second, white women third, 'and everyone else after that'.[56] These priorities have been maintained in the subsequent setting up of the *Daughters of the Dust* website which includes as well as material directly about the film and the Gullah people, hypertext linked material on black independent cinema, and a series of brief memorialisations of black women entitled 'Daughters of the Diaspora'.[57] Dash's hierarchy of audiences marks out the film as a product of civil rights feminism rather than feminist separatism or middle-class feminism. Black women are its primary audience, but they are seen as part of a heterogeneous viewing public. It is through these terms of reference that the film engages with multiple intertwined discourses of identity. Within an overall context of the historical Gullah people, and myths and narratives of African American history, we concentrate here on unpacking some connections between identity constructed according to geography, psychology, faith and gender.

Coincidentally, *Daughters of the Dust* is set in very close proximity to the southern action of *Glory*, around forty years later. By contrast, instead of functioning as battlefield, the South Carolina coast here has a crucial historical function. *Daughters of the Dust* concerns itself with the Gullah or Geechee people of the sea islands of the South, whose geographical isolation has ensured that the population has developed a distinct culture and dialect, such that customs and speech-patterns connect contemporary Gullah to West African culture. The film follows a Gullah family on the eve of their migration north at around the turn of the last century. This context sets up a series of family discussions, memorialisations, rituals and celebrations, and debates over identity, which are focused via a lengthy family picnic. The film climaxes in a series of arguments, reconciliations and a regeneration ceremony.

The overarching issue Dash sets up is the question of the retention of links with Africa, and in particular with the history of women of African descent, over the move from the geographically insulated space of the sea islands. Tensions between a historically conscious Afrocentrism and a turn to white-dominated society in search of betterment is incarnated by the female members of the family. Nana Peazant (Cora Lee Day) as the great-grandmother of the family is the one who most fiercely invokes the importance of links with ancestral African society and culture. The story is narrated by Nana Peazant and by the Unborn Child (Kai-Lynn Warren) who was conceived by rape, and is being carried by Eula Peazant (Alva Rogers) during the time of migration. Eula mediates between Nana's insistence on African heritage, and the members of the family who have already migrated north or are keen to do so. These are Yellow Mary Peazant (Barbara-O), a prostitute, and her girlfriend Trula (Trula Hoosier), visiting from the mainland en route to Trula's birthplace in Nova Scotia; Viola Peazant (Cheryl Lynn Bruce), Yellow Mary's first cousin, and a Baptist missionary who accompanies them on their visit; and Haagar Peazant, described as 'a self-educated progressive striver who desires to leave behind all that ties her family to their African heritage'.[58] All of these latter women have sought empowerment outside the family context and links to Africa, whether through the economics of sex or the adoption of Christian belief to obtain self-esteem, while they are in varying degrees sympathetic to the authority and heritage asserted by Nana. The film features also several males in subsidiary roles: Eula's husband Eli Peazant (Adisa Anderson), Mr Snead, a photographer hired by Viola, the Moslem Bilal Muhammed (Umar Abdurrahamn), and the Cherokee St. Julian Lastchild (M. Cochise Anderson), the lover of Haagar's daughter Iona, who will eventually remain on the island.

The situation of the film in the South Carolina sea islands constitutes an unusual and in many ways unique cultural space. By the time *Daughters of the Dust* was finally made (Dash first began to research the project in 1983 and shooting began in 1987)[59] directors such as Lee and Singleton had firmly established northern post-industrial urban landscape as the definitive setting for filmic narratives of black identity. When Leslie Harris put an African-American female at the centre of such a narrative in *Just Another Girl on the IRT*, she retained the northern urban setting. Obviously *Daughters of the Dust* is related to a very different geography. This is the South, but it is not the South of dominant narratives of the oppression and deprivation of African Americans, the place of slavery to be left by migration northward. The geographical space of the sea islands, as the example of the contemporary Gullahs makes clear, offers a symbolic space after captivity, but before white dominance has erased African social and cultural formations. Yet Dash does not portray the sea islands as offering in any direct way the South as Africa. There are no easy connections with mother Africa in this film. Instead, links have to be made through faith, debate, ritual, and volition. The island setting is also crucial in liberating the female characters from the domestic space to which women are frequently confined in both white and black Hollywood. Domestic space is transformed by the richly coloured sand, vegetation, food and intense sea. All of the shooting of the film is done outside, where all the activity related to working, cooking and eating takes place.

Part of the importance of the symbolic space of the sea islands lies in enabling Dash to construct 'positive images' of life in the rural South, as against the northern urban contexts favoured by the 'new black (mostly male-directed) cinema'. The luscious photography of the picnic food, assembled for the special occasion of the migration to the mainland, offers an alternative and more affirmative history to the overwhelming consciousness of slavery and its legacy. It figures instead the possibilities of African American life in the South in spite of the effects of racial oppression. This project interlocks with another one which breaks more decisively with those logics of positive images which depend heavily on white-centred and androcentric cultural models. The symbolic space of the sea islands is crucial in Dash's re-representation of African American history in enabling her to break with linear narratives of victimisation and heroism, based on white androcentric forms such as the *bildungsroman*. In particular, *Daughters of the Dust* avoids concentrating on the biographical narratives of centred protagonists configured in linear generations: this is not a kind of feminised version of *Roots*. Instead the film evokes a series of such narratives and its narrative interest lies in the tensions between the protagonists. This exclusive concentration on relations between African Americans (with the one exception of St. Julian Lastchild, the one remaining Cherokee on the island) begs the question of how successfully white culture, and in particular the history of white representations of African Americans, can be marginalised or excluded from the film. Dash, hooks, Greg Tate and Bambara have remarked upon the film's project of breaking with stereotypes of African American women and decentring the white patriarchal gaze in order to centre such representations and to render the aesthetic qualities of darker skin.[60]

The film goes still further than this in breaking also with European musical and narrative structures. John Barnes's score deliberately eschews European instruments and structures, using a range of African drums. The sound of batta drums accompanies shots of girls playing on the beach, while talking drums are heard behind the dialogue of some male characters. These could be read as invoking some kind of African authenticity. However, since it is unlikely that most audiences will recognise the music, the drums reference Africa while also implying a cultural gap. If they represent African language, it is a lost language.

In terms of narrative structure, the film eschews linearity, telling and retelling its story from multiple perspectives in a manner analogous to black traditions such as the griots. A binary is set up between the discursive storytelling of Nana Peazant, and the attempts, often comically frustrated, by the photographer Mr Snead to fix and memorialise the islanders in a static image. An issue again here is whether a rejection of European models necessitates the appropriation of, or unwavering affiliation with avant-gardism, 'third world cinema' or a fixed Afra-femcentric aesthetic. Dash foregrounds her debt to and affiliation with such cinemas which were highly influential on university-trained independent African American filmmakers in the 1970s and 1980s, both in personal terms as part of the African diaspora, and also through her use of formal and stylistic modes.[61] Primarily, Dash places herself in the tradition of independent African American cinema. However, her conception of influence is wide-ranging, and on the *Daughters of the Dust* website she lists influences as various as Charles Burnett and Steven Spielberg, African and Latin-American films alongside the work of Eisenstein, Kurosawa and Welles.[62] This marks *Daughters of the Dust* in terms of an emergent film aesthetics that affiliates with 'foreign'-ness but does not step completely outside Hollywood traditions.[63] Thus, for example, Dash's use of the sea may be read as reversing its dominant Hollywood signification of otherness. The sea in *Daughters of the Dust* seems to stand for a symbolic space outside patriarchy, a space of potential for historical and geographical links. It is after all both the route and barrier between the sea islands and Africa. Yet there are continuities here with the symbolic uses of landscape in classic Westerns such as *The Searchers* (John Ford, 1956) and with the representation of the sea in Jane Campion's *The Piano* (New Zealand, 1993), as offering an elemental context for familial relations to be worked through apparently outside existing socio-cultural power structures.

As with the possibilities of integrating female African American identity offered by the symbolic space of the film, Dash also seeks to accommodate patterns of cultural or religious belief which might be considered incommensurable. The Peazant community, who wear the white clothes of the Baptist faith, live in harmony on the island with Moslems. Aside from a certain embarrassment displayed by Viola when describing the Moslem community to the modernist Mr Snead, these relations are presented as unproblematic. But issues of faith constitute some of the most severe tensions between the Peazant protagonists. The central antagonisms here are between Nana Peazant, who tends the gravemarkers and keeps pots of ancestral relics and a tin can of symbolic objects, Haagar Peazant, who wants to leave the traditional and insular Gullah society for the promise of modernity in the north, and Viola Peazant, who is described on the *Daughters of the Dust* website as attempting 'to escape her history and the trauma of her second class citizenship in her Baptist religious beliefs'.[64] These tensions are played out in the film's climactic scenes, during a religious ceremony presided over by Nana Peazant on the eve of the family's departure.

Having stressed the family's need for 'connections', with its members over both time and space, Nana offers what Dash calls 'A Root Revival of Love.'[65] She prepares a 'hand' using a bible and 'scraps of memory' from her tin can. These objects represent non-Christian religious and cultural links with Africa and slave history, though their exact meaning remains obscure. Despite misgivings due to her Baptist belief, Viola is able to kiss the 'hand', as do all of the other Peazants, with one exception. Haagar alone refuses to participate in the ceremony, and bursts out in anger 'Hoodoo ... Hoodoo! Hoodoo mess! Ain't no roots and herbs going to change nothing ... Old Used-To-Do-It-This-Way don't help none today!'

The 'hand', made by lashing together a bible with scraps of African American memory, stands for the unifying narrative of the film. It stages a series of accommodations, such as the welcoming back of the prostitute Yellow Mary despite the disgrace felt by the more censorious or Christianised members of the family, and that between the estranged couple Eula and Eli. These accommodations are themselves interlocked with multiple narratives of personal transformation. Yellow Mary comes to reject the notion of prostitution as a mode of getting on and re-adopts a Gullah identity; Eli has to deal with both his anger and his assumption of patriarchal power with regard to Eula's being 'forced'; while Viola's adoption of white modernist values is questioned and she, like Yellow Mary, comes to accept her affiliation with the Peazant family. The hand's synthesis of different signs of African American history and identity crystallises Dash's practice in the film of seeking to make connections between disparate and often seemingly antagonistic constructions of African American identity. In keeping with this, Dash's emphasis on multiple narratives of transformation has decisively broken with discourses of 'positive images'. None of the protagonists is presented completely sympathetically nor completely unsympathetically. The film implies that there is even a place for the scientific and quantitative approach of Mr Snead; after all, in some senses filmmaking descends from his photographic project.

Viola is a significant figure in this respect. Her articulacy, her desexualised appearance and uptight clothes offer what might be considered a positive image of African American femininity, especially as against the heavily sexualised stereotyping of black women in mainstream Hollywood. Yet her commitment to the modernising force of mainland culture is shown to have to be mediated by connections with the historical experience of African captives, a problem she is presented as painfully coming to terms with.

Eli also begins the film as something of an outsider, in his estrangement from his wife Eula due to her rape and resultant pregnancy. Eli's narrative of psychological development works to illustrate the equivocal position of black men with regard to patriarchal power. His concern about the paternity of the unborn child is represented at the beginning of the film as all-consuming, to such an extent that he cannot help but associate himself with a sense of ownership of Eula's body. This assumption of patriarchal power is far from, but on the same continuum as, that of the rapist. As bell hooks has pointed out, the Peazant women's refusal to identify Eula's assailants to Eli helps to turn him away from oppressive modes of self-empowerment.[66] In large part it is Dash's break with Hollywood grammar that enables this representation of Eli's psychological regeneration. His relationship with Eula is restored through his acceptance of not knowing the identity of her rapist, the father of the unborn child. The audience also forgoes both this knowledge and the satisfaction of a revenge plot which would provide closure for this narrative. While in other respects *Daughters of the Dust* offers narrative resolutions, notably through the series of accommodations described above, the film also suggests through Eli's narrative that resolutions are not always to be sought at the level of form.

Although Eula's rapist is not named, conversation among the Peazant women as to Eli's probable lynching were he to become involved implies that Eula is a direct victim of white patriarchal violence. More debatable is the way in which *Daughters of the Dust* avoids naming Eula's rape, using instead the word 'forced', or being 'ridden'. This represents a

realist representation of women's reaction to rape rather than proclaim-
ing the history of white patriarchal violence.

While Dash throws together the various signs of African American
identities, not all of the protagonists can be or are integrated into the
Peazant extended family. The most obvious example is Yellow Mary's
girlfriend Trula. As part of the foursome, along with Viola and Mr
Snead, returning to the islands at the beginning of the film after life on
the mainland, Yellow Mary and Trula are marked out from the Peazant
family. Their difference is articulated also in their clothing; ostent-
atiously hatted, veiled and parasoled. Like Mr Snead and Viola, the
couple are identified with modernity, emblematised in Yellow Mary's
gift of a tin of factory-made biscuits. Haagar picks on this difference,
articulating it in terms of immorality and the commodification of sex,
and uses it to exclude them: 'Now how's she going to come and put her
shame on Nana Peazant?' During the extended scenes where Yellow
Mary talks to Nana and Haagar's daughters Iona and Myown, and is
eventually welcomed back into the family by Nana, the film often cuts
away to Trula sitting alone and inscrutable on the beach. Most pointedly,
when Yellow Mary is ritually admitted back into the symbolic space of
the islands, the film again cuts to Trula looking on and then moving
away. Dash's script reads, 'Trula does not understand what is happening,
but she realises that Yellow Mary will not be leaving with her the next
morning. Trula runs away from the ceremony.' [67]

For all the psychological narratives of accommodation and regeneration, the ritual enactments of sisterhood and kinship and the pluralistic
representations of African American femininity, the closing scenes of
the film show two distinct groups. While most family members, along
with the visitors, are leaving, the following remain on the island with
the ancestors: Nana Peazant, Eli, Eula and the Unborn Child, Yellow
Mary, St Julian Lastchild and, at the last minute leaving her mother
Haagar to be with her Cherokee lover, Iona. Lostchild, like Trula, has
not participated in Nana Peazant's unifying ceremony, and the final
scene is presented in such a way that Lostchild and Iona are separated
from the rest of the islanders – they ride off on his horse. What is to
be made of these exclusions? Undoubtedly they could be read in terms
of privileging the Peazant bloodline, and thereby as an essentialist
reading of African heritage which excludes from the community not
only the Cherokee but also Trula. Unlike Yellow Mary, Trula does
not renounce the commodified, consumerist ethic associated with the

mainland during the course of the film. Nevertheless, considered as Yellow Mary's lesbian lover (a relationship that is strongly implied), her exclusion follows a logic of blood relation predicated on reproduction and heterosexuality.

We would suggest that, given the formal strategies employed in the film with respect to Eli and Eula, the final leaving scene is best viewed as providing a provisional closure to the narrative that interacts dynamically with audience investments and desires. *Daughters of the Dust* need not pretend that a complete resolution was possible in 1902, and indeed audience members' potential identification with the excluded Trula might make for a more energetic response than a historically bogus inclusiveness. Such a dynamic relation between pasts and presents, neither of which are static, is supported by the last of the film's words, in which the Unborn Child recollects, 'We remained behind, growing older, wiser, and stronger'.

Iconicity: Image and Narrative in Spike Lee's *Malcolm X*

The iconicity of Malcolm X, not to mention his reputation while alive, has polarised opinion both within and between racialised positions. Even before Lee's film was made, controversy surrounded his demand that white director Norman Jewison be removed from the project; then subsequently, his own installation as director was challenged by prominent black critics such as Amiri Baraka, Armond White and Stanley Crouch.[68] The ongoing debate over Malcolm X's legacy to black Americans spawned several book-length studies of his iconicity and cultural symbolism in the 1990s, the best of which, Joe Wood's *Malcolm X: In Our Own Image*, appeared while Lee's lengthy pre-release publicity campaign was putting the X emblem on T-shirts, jackets, caps, baseball hats and potato chips.[69] Such was the intensity of these disputes that in a review of the film in *New Republic*, Stanley Kauffmann was able to imply that it was the proprietary behaviour of black critics that had delayed its production, since 'a white sponsor has been on hand for twenty-five years.'[70] This was the length of time that had elapsed between white producer Marvin Worth's optioning the Alex Haley-ghosted *The Autobiography of Malcolm X* and the film finally starting production. By contrast, and more convincingly, Ed Guerrero blames this delay on the potentially disruptive effects of X's narrative on dominant representations of race. For Guerrero, 'the Malcolm X project had been systematically repressed' by virtue of being 'held in studio purgatory for twenty-five years'. He goes on to quote David Bradley, one of the legion of scriptwriters hired and fired: the studio 'didn't keep firing writers because the scripts were wrong. They kept firing writers because the *story* was wrong.' [71]

There are several reasons for the intensity of disputes over X's meaning. The inflammatory rhetoric of racial separatism he employed while speaking on behalf of Elijah Muhammad's Nation of Islam is an obvious one, but more relate to his positioning in relation to not one but two modes of black politics: his twelve-year period in the Nation of Islam from 1952 to 1964, and the last eleven months of his life when he had formally broken with Muhammad though remained a Moslem. As Joe Wood, among others, has pointed out, the sheer power of X's image, disseminated through a range of commodified means, has added to the pluralisation of its meaning. [72]

Interpretations of X have also been crucial in representations of black politics post-civil rights, where Malcolm X has functioned as one half of a binary opposition with Martin Luther King, an arrangement which falsifies both X's later, conciliatory moves towards other black leaders and King's developing critiques of capitalism after the escalation of the Vietnam War and the Watts riots. Ed Guerrero and Carol Cooper have argued that in a film such as *A Soldier's Story* (Norman Jewison, 1984), a King/X binary is invoked in order to discredit the separatist ideology associated with one Pte. Peterson (played by Denzel Washington), and to validate the aspirational black yuppieism of Lt. Davenport (Edward Rollins). [73] For Guerrero, the film's invocation of the King/X dichotomy serves to privilege the upwardly striving and individualistic black male against the interests of what he calls 'the black collectivity'. It is not hard to see how the polarisation of the politics of King and X works here and elsewhere in the service of white dominance.

Spike Lee's invocation of the King/X binary in his 1989 film *Do the Right Thing* is more ambiguous. During the film, a handicapped character known as Smiley hands out a photograph of Martin Luther King and Malcolm X shaking hands. In the action of the film, this implied possibility of a synthetic and productive black unity is closed off. To sum up very reductively, racial tensions erupt and break out of control at the end of the film. Black anger is deployed in burning down Sal's pizzeria rather than employing the tried and tested techniques of consumer boycott. Lee inserts into the closing titles two antithetical quotations, one from King and the other from X. The question here is whether these are read as a call for synthesis, as Lee has suggested,[74] or a sardonic commentary on the preceding action, which seems to suggest that there is no way of resolving their polarisation.

In the 1990s there emerged some significant ways of describing Malcolm X that implied the possibility of resolving this polarisation. A crucial term in these is an emphasis on X's 'humanity'. Distancing X from the black separatist politics that brought him to national prominence, such discourses stress both the openness to self-criticism and to change demonstrated by X's two conversion experiences, and the potential demonstrated in his last year for unifying anti-racism. Concentrating on the biographical narrative, black conservative Shelby Steele has commented that 'The life of Malcolm X touched so many human archetypes that his story seems to supersede any racial context ...'.[75] Comparably, Joe Wood describes X's two revelations as 'first, his embrace of his Black Muslim identity; second, the embrace of human commonality.' [76] These two great sequential shifts in position that make up X's career as commonly understood [77] set up the potential and the difficulty of representing X as a liberatory black figure. Taken together, the two 'embraces' listed by Wood imply the possibility of constructing a 'black humanity', which breaks with the hierarchised black/white binary identified by Cornel West above. Yet the sequentiality of these revelatory shifts might also be taken to imply the mutual exclusivity of blackness and a notion of humanity still dominated by white power.

Lee's decision to base the film on the *Autobiography* makes it difficult to represent African American identities in relational and historically dynamic modes such as those set up in *Daughters of the Dust*. For strategic reasons, the *Autobiography* is constructed around what X calls in a speech used in the film, two 'St Paul' type conversions. The first, relating to his recruitment to the Nation of Islam while in prison, dramatises first the degrading effects of racism on African Americans, and then the crucial importance of the Nation of Islam in allowing blacks human dignity. The second was his renunciation of black separatism following his establishment of brotherly relations with Moslems of non-black appearance during a hajj, or pilgrimage, to Mecca, undertaken after his suspension from the Nation. This happened while Haley and X were working on the *Autobiography*, and is not fully integrated into it. Essentially, Lee's film follows this narrative structure with almost no concession to later research.[78] What this determines is a biographical narrative structured so as to be strong on images but short on explanation. Lee's film follows the *Autobiography* in representing X's changes of political position as the finding of 'truth through revelation', or in terms of 'psychic conversion', as Joe Wood and Cornel West describe the narrative.[79] Thereby X's biographical narrative is structured as a series of iconic images, negating the mode of explanation. Instead of offering then a historical dynamic, the film represents X's story as a series of moments.

The film also negates the relational constructions of identity that were again apparent in *Daughters of the Dust*, or rather, to be more specific, it represents determinant relations of identity as unidirectional, centring on father/son relationships. Early in the film, flashbacks introduce X's father, a Garveyite preacher represented being harassed and eventually killed by white racists. The experiences of the young Malcolm Little (Denzel Washington) are offered via flashback and voice-over as explanations for such things as his sexual use of white women during his career as Detroit Red. Red's underworld activities are underwritten for a while by a surrogate father in the form of West Indian Archie (Delroy Lindo). On his conversion, Elijah Muhammad becomes a more powerful and revelatory/saving father, though eventually, as with West Indian Archie, Malcolm breaks with him. In the final phase of the film X is touted as a father-figure himself. The film shows him describing in a speech the caring and responsible nature of fatherhood, and nurturing young African American men into the ways of the Nation of Islam, many of whom follow him with filial devotion after the break with Elijah Muhammad. To one of these, sent by Elijah Muhammad to booby-trap his car, X says, 'I won't let myself come between you and your father,' to which Sidney replies, 'You are my father.' One or two eventually betray him as X did to several of his own father-figures. In this final phase, the film sets up X as not simply offering African Americans unconditional love (as many commentators have described him, including West in the article quoted above), but also in the terms used by Paul Gilroy, as 'a patriarchal sign in the family romance that black political history has become'.[80]

The construction of Malcolm X as a paternalistic figure does not in itself determine the scope of the film's representation of history as dynamic, nor does it necessarily cement the film into a static representation of the patriarchal structures of the Nation of Islam. As several critics have pointed out in different ways, Lee uses his trademark stylistic innovations to undercut and to defamiliarise the realist historicism of the Hollywood biopic.[81] Jonathan Scott Lee has argued that the film contains several scenes that can be read as 'mistakes' or 'cinematic parapraxes' which offer to deconstruct it as a closed semantic statement and enlist the audience in a project of constructing the meaning of Malcolm X.[82] Analogously, Lisa Kennedy has commented that 'Lee's greatest legacy has been his refusal of closure', pointing to a dialectic in his films between 'Lee the ideologue', intent on delivering a message which is consistently undercut by 'the desire of Lee the artist/activist to render the world in all its messiness'.[83] Undoubtedly, there are some cinematic effects in *Malcolm X* which do undercut biopic realist historicism: the use of different film stocks, freeze-frames, and such innovations as the unusual travelling shot from below, used earlier by Lee and cinematographer Ernest Dickerson in *Jungle Fever* and later in *Clockers*. In the latter a character, in this case Malcolm walking to his last fatal rally, appears to be static while the background moves behind him. However, none of these undercut or offer the possibility to rethink the patriarchalism of the Nation of Islam or the paternalism of dominant constructions of Malcolm X.

Ed Guerrero, in a nuanced response to the film, also celebrates its use of cinematic effects as a means of negotiating the relation between straight biographical narrative and historical contextualisation. By themselves, each would either exaggerate or negate individual human agency. Instead, Guerrero argues that through innovations such as the juxtaposition of 'slick, poster-bright colours' with grainy film stock, and the casting of special guests such as the New York activist Rev. Al Sharpton and Black Panther co-founder Bobby Seale as two street speakers vying with Malcolm for attention, Lee's film manages both to celebrate the life of Malcolm X and to position it with respect to what Guerrero calls 'the insistent, intervening power of history.'[84] However, it seems equally possible that the not only larger but also more intense than life representation of X, as compared with grainy black and white images of the 'real' X, King, and JFK might serve to fetishise Malcolm. At the same time, while the juxtaposition of Washington as X with Sharpton and Seale offers an image of unity across historical and political divides, it decontextualises and dehistoricises their actual positions and struggles so as to negate the hard work of negotiation and compromise in achieving unity.

By itself, as we have said, the film's one-dimensional representation of Malcolm X according to the frame of paternalism need not lock it into the political impasse X himself faced on his return from Mecca. However, because Lee's *Malcolm X* remains structurally in thrall to the myth of X as the best father, an icon on which none of its de-familiarising strategies are brought to bear, the film ultimately follows X's trajectory. Cornel West's essay quoted from above implies that, following his psychic conversion experience on the hajj, Malcolm never resolved the problem of maintaining black unity, having abandoned a belief in black separatism. For West, this problem can be resolved by conceiving of blackness in terms of cultural hybridity, but he advances several reasons why X was resistant to this resolution.[85] The closest X came to such a notion was his contacts with African leaders and his preparedness to make strategic alliances with other black and radical groups in America.

Angela Y. Davis has argued for a transformation of the legacy of Malcolm X's final year from a 'backward and imprisoning memory' into a 'forward-looking impetus for creative political thinking and organizing'.[86] In trying to think through some of the implications of the positions taken up by him after the return from Mecca, she claims that there was space here for black feminism. Another means of resolving such an impasse as that described by West would be to critique the paternalism of the Nation of Islam itself and of separatist discourses in general. This would unmask them as merely reversing the discourses of white supremacy, and further the project of syn-thesising feminist and black politics. Lee's *Malcolm X* is so committed to the iconicity of Malcolm as the great father-figure that it does little to engage with Davis's suggestion. The film does range well outside the scope of the *Autobiography* in showing the courtship and domestic life of Malcolm and Betty Shabazz (played by Angela Bassett). However, even when tensions between the couple are represented, the scenes are constructed in such a way as to reinscribe the public/private dichotomy. Instead of any kind of dynamic between feminist and black liberation, the film represents Malcolm's domestic situation in terms of the negative effects of his public career on the family. Conscious of the effects of his long absences, the stress caused by threats, and attacks on the family home, at one point Malcolm apologises to Betty for being a poor husband and father. But such representations do nothing to inter-rogate patriarchal structures, instead reinscribing the androcentric narrative of paternalism. Effectively, the film suggests that what Betty and the children lose in terms of a paternalist figure is gained by the black community in general. Lee historically misrepresents both the form and the significance of Betty's relationship with Malcolm. He has her talking back in ways which no black Moslem woman would have been allowed to do; while what is not shown in the film are Betty's more significant and independent actions in leaving Malcolm three times.[87]

Lee's film does seem to be committed to a project analogous to that called for by Davis, but its failure to come to terms with racial hybridity or gender politics undermines the production of a historically dynamic narrative of Malcolm X's significance. The film claims humanity for Malcolm X while refusing dominant, white-inflected notions of humanity. But rather than routeing this problematic through a self-conscious interrogation of gender, Lee's film remains firmly within the compass of the definition of Malcolm X as 'our *manhood*, our living black manhood' made by Ossie Davis in his funeral eulogy. It is this manhood, Ossie Davis suggests, that demands honouring: 'This was his best meaning to his people, and in honouring him we honour the best in ourselves.' Placing Davis's eulogy at the end of his book-of-the-film, Lee implies that this defines its scope.

The last section of the film, after X's assassination, does attempt to represent Malcolm X's significance in terms of a historical dynamic. It is composed of a series of images, of X and others, which culminate in intercutting between Harlem and Soweto. In one sequence a crowd of South African blacks are shown carrying posters of Malcolm X during a street demonstration. This is followed by a series of head and shoulder shots of schoolchildren in Harlem and Soweto, who one by one announce directly to camera 'I am Malcolm X'. Finally, Nelson Mandela, as the teacher in the Soweto classroom, speaks the film's final speech. Here the film makes its last play to consolidate both a notion of Malcolm X as some kind of father-figure to the Afro-diasporic community, and to sustain a sense of the forward-looking impetus of his legacy called for by Davis and West. As such, the scene is only partially successful. The displacement from Harlem to South Africa is made presumably in order to indicate both the global diasporic scope of X's paternity and the historical dynamic of black liberation. However, it serves only to underline the film's failure to articulate a dynamic sense of X's legacy for African Americans. Moreover, this conclusion not only turns the film back into a retrospective contemplation of gains made (as articulated in Mandela's speech), but also is in itself open to charges of cultural imperialism. Lee's tacking on of South African history to the biopic of Malcolm X offers up a narrative of American history as paradigmatic of global history. Paradoxically, the effect of this is to de-racialise X and resituate him according to the equation between America and the world made in the multiculturalist sci-fi movie *Independence Day* (Roland Emmerich, 1996).[88]

Having followed the *Autobiography* in minimising or omitting Malcolm X's visits to Egypt, Saudi Arabia, the Sudan, Nigeria and Ghana in 1959, and to Nigeria, Ghana, Liberia, Senegal and Morocco in 1965, Lee's film fails to establish a narrative link with the African diaspora. The link is made, but via the historically and imperialistically suspect means of having the children of Soweto brandish X's image. The film does use images brilliantly at times to crystallise political issues, none more so than in the opening titles, which intercut footage of the Rodney King beating with the burning down of the Stars and Stripes into a huge X. The sequence provides at once a political message about the historical dynamic of black oppression and resistance, while at the same time it demonstrates the symbiosis between visibility and power. Without the video footage of the beating, Rodney King would have been just another statistic. This powerful and successful engagement with iconicity, however, tends to negate the possibilities for a dynamic representation of X's legacy.

Through their historicising of the construction of ethnic identity and pluralising of images of African Americans, the films we have been discussing have left a legacy which can be seen in such mainstream projects as Carl Franklin's *Devil in a Blue Dress* (1996). Set in the 1940s it represents a black private investigator Easy Rawlins (Denzel Washington) as a strong, eroticised figure explicitly contained economically and ideologically by the institutions of the workplace and the police, but heroically overcoming them. The film's focus on post-war racism in Los Angeles by employers and police force and the problematics and exoticism of passing in both white and black communnities can be read as both reclaiming African American identity in this period and explicating reasons for the civil rights movements. Still, we would not maintain that this strategy is without risks, nor that the mainstream acceptance of actors such as Washington signals a complete break with the negative imaging of the past. Also, as we will now argue, the advances in representing ethnic identity seen in *Glory*, *Malcolm X* and *Daughters of the Dust* are reliant to varying extents on the stabilising and normative representation of heterosexuality.

Notes

1. Richard Dyer, 'White', *Screen* 29/4 (1988), pp. 44–64; p. 45.
2. Herman Gray, *Watching Race: Television and the Struggle for Blackness* (Minneapolis: University of Minnesota Press, 1995), pp. 162–3.
3. W. E. B. Du Bois, *The Souls of Black Folk* (New York: Bantam, 1989); Toni Morrison, *Playing in the Dark: Whiteness and the Literary Imagination* (Cambridge, MA: Harvard University Press, 1992); Robert Gooding-Williams, 'Look, a negro!' in Robert Gooding-Williams (ed.), *Reading Rodney King/Reading Urban Uprising* (New York and London: Routledge, 1993), pp. 157–77.
4. Gooding-Williams, 'Look, a negro!', p. 158.
5. See Cornel West, 'The new cultural politics of difference', in Russell Ferguson, Martha Gever, Trinh T. Minh-ha, and Cornel West (eds), *Out There: Marginalization and Contemporary Cultures* (Cambridge: MIT Press, 1990), pp. 19–36, discussed in more detail below.
6. See Thomas R. Cripps, '*The Birth of a Race* company: An early stride toward a Black cinema', *Journal of Negro History* 59 (January 1974), pp. 28–37.
7. See the simplistic and compromised but indicative account in William K. Everson, *American Silent Film* (New York: Oxford University Press, 1978), pp. 83–5.
8. Everson, *Silent Film*, p. 84.
9. See James Snead, Colin MacCabe and Cornel West (eds), *White Screens/Black Images: Hollywood from the Dark Side* (New York and London: Routledge, 1994), especially 'Spectatorship and capture in *King Kong*: The guilty look', pp. 1–28.
10. Daniel J. Leab, *From Sambo to Superspade: The Black Experience in Motion Pictures* (Boston: Houghton Mifflin, 1975); Donald Bogle, *Toms, Coons, Mulattoes, Mammies, and Bucks: An Interpretive History of Blacks in American Films* (New York: Viking Press, 1973); Thomas Cripps, *Slow Fade to Black: The Negro in American Film, 1900–1942* (New York: Oxford University Press, 1977).
11. Snead, *White Screens/Black Images*, pp. 1–2.
12. Snead, *White Screens/Black Images*, pp. 2–3.
13. Snead, *White Screens/Black Images*, p. viii.
14. Mark A. Reid, *Redefining Black Film* (Berkeley: University of California Press, 1993); Manthia Diawara, 'Black American cinema: The new realism', in Manthia Diawara (ed.), *Black American Cinema* (New York and London: Routledge, 1993), pp. 3–25.
15. Reid, *Redefining Black Film*, p. 1.
16. See Reid, *Redefining Black Film*, pp. 2–4, n. 35, p. 150; and pp. 132–6.
17. Compare for example the 1971 films *Sweet Sweetback's Baadasssss Song* written and directed by and starring Melvin Van Peebles, who also wrote the music, and *Shaft*, directed by Gordon Parks, edited by Hugh A. Robertson and starring Richard Roundtree, with music by Isaac Hayes. According to Reid, control of the essential aspects of the production of *Shaft* was exercised by the white scenarist, producer and executive producers, respectively Ernest Tidyman, Joel Freeman, Sterling Silliphant and Roger Lewis. Reid goes further, arguing that the fact that *Sweetback* was distributed by what he calls a 'mini-major distribution company' bars it from

consideration as an independent African-American film. See Reid, *Redefining Black Film*, p. 83.

18. Diawara, 'Black American cinema', p. 3.

19. Diawara, 'Black American cinema', pp. 9–11, 13.

20. Diawara, 'Black American cinema', p. 12.

21. Many of the films canonised in Diawara's list of black independent film would be excluded from Reid's definition of independence, due to their distribution by non-black organisations. See Reid, *Redefining Black Film*, n. 35, p. 150.

22. For an acerbic critique of *Dead Poets Society* which lives up to its title, see the section 'Dead white male heterosexual poets society' in Tania Modleski, *Feminism Without Women: Culture and Criticism in a 'Post-feminist' Age*, pp. 137–40.

23. The statement opens Clyde Taylor's article 'Decolonizing the image: New U. S. black cinema', in Peter Steven (ed.), *Jump Cut: Hollywood, Politics and Counter Cinema* (New York: Praeger, 1985), pp. 166–78.

24. For such an interrogation of discourses of authenticity in Lee's films and their critical reception, see Wahneema Lubiano, 'But compared to what?: Reading realism, representation, and essentialism in *School Daze, Do the Right Thing*, and the Spike Lee discourse', *Black American Literature Forum* 25/2, pp. 253–81.

25. West, 'New cultural politics', p. 29; Henry Louis Gates, Jr., 'The blackness of blackness: A critique of the sign of the signifying monkey', in Henry Louis Gates, Jr. (ed.), *Black Literature and Literary Theory* (New York: Methuen, 1984), pp. 287–321; p. 297.

26. West, 'New cultural politics', p. 29.

27. West, 'New cultural politics', p. 29.

28. West, 'New cultural politics', p. 20.

29. John Leland with Andrew Murr, Mark Miller, Farai Chideya and Abigail Kuflik, 'New Jack Cinema enters screening: With 19 films this year, Hollywood fades to black', *Newsweek*, 10 June, 1991, pp. 50–2; p. 50. As Ed Guerrero points out in his extended and very useful discussion of this issue, estimates of the black movie audience, usually invoked during recessionary periods, tend to vary between 25 and 30 per cent. See 'Chapter 5: Black film in the 1990s: The new black movie boom and its portents', Ed Guerrero, *Framing Blackness: the African American Image in Film* (Philadelphia: Temple University Press, 1993), pp. 157–214; especially pp. 164–8.

30. See Jesse Algeron Rhines, 'The political economy of black film', *Cineaste*, 21/3 (1995), pp. 38–9.

31. See for example the roundtable discussion 'Color bars', featuring Charles Fuller, Richard Wesley, John Sayles and Reginald Hudlin in *American Film*, April 1988, pp. 37–42, and the cover stories Betsy Sharkey, 'Knocking on Hollywood's door: Black filmmakers like Spike Lee struggle to see and be seen', *American Film*, July/August 1989, pp. 22–7, 52, 54 and Thulani Davis, 'Local hero: workin' 40 acres and a mule in Brooklyn', op. cit., pp. 26–7.

32. Leland et al., 'New Jack cinema', *Newsweek*, 10 June, 1991, pp. 50–2.

33. See for example Stanley Kauffmann on John Singleton and Matty Rich in 'Stanley Kauffmann on films', *The New Republic*, 23 May, 1994, pp. 34–5.

34. See Rhines, 'Political economy', p. 39.

35. Henry A. Giroux, 'Living dangerously: Identity politics and the new cultural racism: Towards a critical pedagogy of representation', *Cultural Studies* 7/1 (1993), pp. 1–27; p. 5.

36. See for example Rush H. Limbaugh III, *The Way Things Ought To Be* ([1992] New York: Star, 1993), Chapter 18, 'Multiculturalism', pp. 205–14.

37. Giroux, 'Living dangerously', pp. 14–15.

38. Giroux, 'Living dangerously', p. 16.

39. Giroux, 'Living dangerously', p. 16.

40. K. Anthony Appiah, ' "No bad nigger": Blacks as the ethical principle in the movies', in Marjorie Garber, Jann Matlock and Rebecca L. Walkowitz (eds), *Media Spectacles* (London and New York: Routledge, 1993), pp. 77–90; pp. 81–2.

41. Appiah, ' "No bad nigger" ', p. 83.

42. Appiah, ' "No bad nigger" ', p. 81.

43. Snead, *White Screens/Black Images*, p. 2. In the Foreword to *White Screens/Black Images* Colin MacCabe argues that Snead's untimely death forestalled his analysis of the developments under discussion here (ibid., pp. viii–ix.)

44. Robert Gooding-Williams, 'Black cupids, white desires: Reading the recoding of racial difference in *Casablanca*', in Werner Sollors and Maria Diedrich (eds), *The Black Columbiad: Defining Moments in African American Literature and Culture* (Cambridge and London: Harvard University Press, 1994), pp. 201–11. Gooding-Williams focuses specifically on Thomas Cripps's *Slow Fade to Black* (New York: Oxford University Press, 1977).

45. Gooding-Williams, 'Black cupids, white desires', p. 202.

46. West, 'New cultural politics', p. 29.

47. Herman Gray has written persuasively of the need to understand the persistence of essentialism and androcentric nationalism in terms of their cultural and class location, alongside a recognition of the privileges of academic sites. See Herman Gray, 'African American political desire and the seductions of contemporary cultural politics', *Cultural Studies* 7 (1993), pp. 364–73.

48. See Michele Wallace, '*Boyz N the Hood* and *Jungle Fever*', in Gina Dent (ed.), *Black Popular Culture* (Seattle: Bay Press, 1992), pp. 123–31.

49. bell hooks, *Outlaw Culture* (New York and London: Routledge, 1994), p. 116.

50. *The True Story of Glory Continues* (Ben Burtt, 1991), available on selected video cassettes of *Glory*.

51. Ella Shohat and Robert Stam, *Unthinking Eurocentrism: Multiculturalism and the Media* (London and New York: Routledge, 1994), pp. 4–5.

52. Civil War historian James M. McPherson argues that the film falsifies the precise composition of the 54th in order to make it more typical of the racial compositions of Northern regiments in the Civil War. See James M. McPherson, 'Glory', in Mark C. Carnes (general ed.), *Past Imperfect: History According to the Movies* ([1995]New York: Cassell, 1996), pp. 128–31; p. 130.

53. James M. McPherson reads this scene as a coded reference to 'the "darky" stereotype' in *Glory*, p. 131.

54. Giroux, 'Living dangerously', p. 16.

55. See Toni Cade Bambara, 'Preface', in Julie Dash with Toni Cade Bambara and bell hooks, *Daughters Of The Dust: The Making of an African American Woman's Film* (New York: New Press, 1992), pp. xi–xvi; Toni Cade Bambara, 'Reading the signs, empowering the eye: *Daughters Of The Dust* and the black independent cinema movement', in Manthia Diawara (ed.), *Black American Cinema*, pp. 118–44; Ed Guerrero, *Framing Blackness: The African American Image in Film* (Philadelphia: Temple University Press, 1993), pp. 169, 175–7; and Diawara, 'Black American Cinema: The new realism', discussed above.

56. 'Dialogue between bell hooks and Julie Dash April 26, 1992', Dash, *Daughters Of The Dust*, pp. 27–67; p. 40.

57. The address of the *Daughters of the Dust* website is http://www. pacificnet. net/~geechgirl.

58. This and the other brief character descriptions are drawn largely from the website pages, where the protagonists are also related to the deities of West African cosmologies.

59. Julie Dash, 'Making *Daughters Of The Dust*', Dash, *Daughters Of The Dust*, pp. 1–25; pp. 5, 7.

60. See hooks and Dash, 'Dialogue', pp. 40–2; Greg Tate, 'A word from Greg Tate', in Dash, *Daughters Of The Dust*, pp. 69–71; p. 70; and Bambara, 'Reading the signs', passim.

61. See hooks and Dash, 'Dialogue', pp. 65–6.

62. 'Histories and influences: African American cinema and more', http://www. pacificnet. net/~geechgirl/History. html.

63. See hooks and Dash, 'Dialogue', p. 66.

64. http://www. pacificnet. net/~geechgirl/TheFilm. html.

65. Julie Dash, 'The script', Dash, *Daughters Of The Dust* , pp. 75–168; p. 158.

66. hooks and Dash, 'Dialogue', p. 50.

67. Dash, 'Script', p. 160.

68. Lee's defence is summarised in Guerrero, *Framing Blackness*, pp. 198–99. For a typical example of Lee's long-running disagreements with Crouch, see Spike Lee, 'Doing the job' (interview with James Verniere), *Sight and Sound* 3/2 (February 1993), pp. 10–11; p. 11.

69. Joe Wood (ed.), *Malcolm X: In Our Own Image* (New York: St. Martin's Press, 1992); see also Eric Michael Dyson, *Making Malcolm: The Myth and Meaning of Malcolm X* (New York and Oxford: Oxford University Press, 1994).

70. Stanley Kauffmann on films: 'The fire that time', *The New Republic*, 207/26 (21 December 1992), pp. 26–7; p. 27.

71. Guerrero, *Framing Blackness*, pp. 197, 198.

72. Joe Wood, 'Malcolm X and the new blackness', in Wood, *Malcolm X*, pp. 1–17; many contributors to Wood's volume preface their remarks by registering the proliferation and commodification of X's image and significance.

73. Carol Cooper, ' "Soldier's Story" salute', *Film Comment*, November/December 1984, p. 17; Guerrero, *Framing Blackness*, pp. 135–6.

74. Lee and Verniere, 'Doing the job', p. 10.

75. Shelby Steele, '*Malcolm X*', *The New Republic* 207:26 (21 December 1992), pp. 27–32; p. 28.

76. Wood, 'The new blackness', p. 10.

77. For another version of this narrative of three phases separated by two revelations see Kauffmann, 'The fire that time', p. 26.

78. The major source excluded is Bruce Perry, *Malcolm: The Life of a Man Who Changed Black America* (New York: Station Hill Press, 1991), an admittedly iconoclastic text which infuriated Amiri Baraka as much as Lee. See Amiri Baraka, 'Malcolm as ideology', in Wood, *Malcolm X*, pp. 18–35, passim.

79. Wood, 'The new blackness', p. 10; Cornel West, 'Malcolm X and black rage', in Wood, *Malcolm X*, pp. 48–58; pp. 49, 50, 52, 53. Wood's description refers to the *Autobiography* representation, while West is discussing what he thinks of as the actual trajectory of X's thought.

80. Paul Gilroy, 'Introduction', *Small Acts: Thoughts on the Politics of Black Cultures* (London: Serpents Tail, 1993), pp. 1–15; p. 13.
81. By 'realist historicism' we do not mean of course that Hollywood biopics have sought to achieve historical accuracy, but to suggest that they are fully committed to modes of representation that claim historical accuracy.
82. Jonathan Scott Lee, 'Spike Lee's *Malcolm X* as transformational object', *American Imago* 52/2 (1995), pp. 155–67; p. 158 and passim.
83. See Lisa Kennedy, 'Is *Malcolm X* the right thing?', *Sight and Sound* 3/2 (February 1993), pp. 6–10; p. 9.
84. Guerrero, *Framing Blackness*, pp. 201–2.
85. West, 'Malcolm X and black rage', pp. 54–5.
86. Angela Y. Davis, 'Meditations on the legacy of Malcolm X', in Wood, *Malcolm X*, pp. 36–47; pp. 44–5.
87. Betty Shabazz is quoted in Davis, 'Meditations', p. 44.
88. See conclusion for further discussion of *Independence Day*.

CHAPTER 3

Putting the Homo into America: Reconstructing Gay Identities in the National Frame

In his affectionate interpretive history of blacks in film, *Toms, Coons, Mulattoes, Mammies and Bucks,* Donald Bogle says that 'the essence of black film history is not found in the stereotyped role but in what certain talented actors have done with the stereotype'. In the same sense, the characters created by Pangborn, Sutton, Horton, Webb and dozens of others brought a brief electric contact with the quicksilver truth and wrought a comic chaos that the social order suppressed. Each in his own style, they were signposts to a hidden gay experience where chaos was the norm.

Vito Russo, The Celluloid Closet [1]

Just as recent work on images of blacks and women has done, thinking about images of gayness needs to go beyond simply dismissing stereotypes as wrong and distorted. Righteous dismissal does not make the stereotypes go away, and tends to prevent us from understanding just what stereotypes are, how they function, ideologically and aesthetically, and why they are so resilient in the face of our rejection of them.

Richard Dyer, 'Stereotyping' [2]

It puts the homo back in Homicide.

'Teaser' for Swoon (Tom Kalin, 1992)

As in the previous chapters, we are concerned here not with films as revelative of specific identities, but as articulating forms of identity in symbolic terms. Our approach to discussing sexuality in film therefore is not determined by notions of 'gay film' and 'lesbian film' but instead is generated by a multifaceted concern with filmic representations of gay and lesbian identity. The groundbreaking work of Vito Russo has uncovered a history of gay representations in mainstream cinema, in ways similar to the work done on African American representations by scholars such as Bogle, Cripps, Leab and others in the 1970s. As Russo's explicit alignment with Bogle, quoted above, implies, the criteria for reading these representations derived from similar sources, notably the impetus to distinguish between positive and negative images which came from the culturalist turn of the black civil rights movement and the post-Stonewall liberation movements respectively. And also like the work on African American representations, registered presciently as above by Richard Dyer, these parameters have been problematised by critical work in the 1980s and 1990s. Two major interpolations can be traced. First, debates over the efficacy of positive imagery for the lesbian/gay audience, critic and filmmaker. Second, the fragmentation of politicised identities based on sexual object-choice due to the increased visibility and activism associated with lesbian consumers and producers after Stonewall, and also latterly because of the developments around the term 'queer'.

Hence, though the critical paradigms of African American and gay criticism can be aligned it would be oversimplistic to see them as having identical trajectories. Part of the reason for this has been and remains the fluidity of lesbian and gay identity which may take forms as radically different as 'out' gay and lesbian identification, individual sex acts, and same-sex bonding, or combinations of the above. There are parallels between this instability and the notions of African American identity as hybridity and as jazz, put forward by Cornel West and Henry Louis Gates Jr., and also with the cross-cutting of ethnic identity by gender, sexuality, generational, regional and other forms of identity. However, a major differentiating factor lies in the complex issue of lesbian and gay visibility.

Even given the vast energy put into such a project by the political right in the USA, it remains impossible to read an individual's sexuality directly from their appearance. The question of visibility is crucial for both lesbians/gays and for straights and has given rise to a series of cultural productions including the coded forms of sexual and gendered display in stereotypes of gay and lesbian identity, such as the sissy, camp and drag. For gays and lesbians, the coding of forms of sexual identity has fulfilled a crucial function not only for intra-communal recognition, but also in playing with or contesting straight normativity. While there are parallels here with the notion of 'passing' for African Americans and other non-white ethnicities, and with the uses of black ethnicity to normalise non-black identity as discussed in the previous chapter, in general, mainstream and subcultural constructions of gay and lesbian identity have been more dynamically interlaced and imbricated together than have racialised and ethnic representations. As Alan Sinfield has put it, 'while in some instances race and ethnicity are not manifest, for lesbians and gay men passing is almost unavoidable'.[3] In fact the focusing on stereotypes by gays and straights alike is profoundly double, functioning both to police and to fracture white straight normativity.

This doubleness has provoked a certain trajectory in gay and lesbian criticism emerging after Russo's book, which has attempted to stabilise resistive readings of mainstream Hollywood by locating histories of the consumption of images rather than their production. Thus, for example, Al LaValley argued in 1985 that:

> There exists another gay history of the movies that has little to do with gay themes and characters, yet constitutes a major part of gay consciousness, both before and after the watershed Stonewall riots of 1969. In the many years of absence of any real representation of themselves on screen, gays created this history out of straight or nominally straight films.[4]

For LaValley, the pleasures of making coded readings of gay identity in mainstream film are no substitute for the more recent positive images discourses such as that of the 'natural man', but neither is their persistence to be read in terms of the nostalgia criticised heavily in Russo.[5] Instead, LaValley argues, it is precisely the elements of stereotypical codification that speak to that which is playful, utopian and transformative in gay culture.[6]

This excavating of alternative histories of consumption has coexisted slightly uneasily with a continuing sense of the instability of heterosexuality as constructed by Hollywood, and the uses of constructions of homosexuality to stabilise it. As Diana Fuss has argued, the production of gay and lesbian stereotypes in mainstream culture can be regarded as showing the strains of the white straight centre trying to define what it is not:

> For heterosexuality to achieve the status of the 'compulsory,' it must present itself as a practice governed by some internal necessity. The language and law that regulates the establishment of heterosexuality

as both an identity and an institution, both a practice and a system, is the language and law of defence and protection: heterosexuality secures its self-identity and shores up its ontological boundaries by protecting itself from what it sees as the continual predatory encroachments of its contaminated other, homosexuality.[7]

Fuss thus explains the continuing use of representations of homosexuality as deviant and as inherently linked to criminality, and thus symbolically opposed to, while being constitutive of, dominant representations of heterosexuality as normative and lawful.

Such uses are particularly evident in early 1990s thrillers such as *The Silence of the Lambs* (Jonathan Demme, 1991) and *Basic Instinct* (Paul Verhoeven, 1992), where the law and the institutions of heterosexuality are represented as under threat from the deviant and murderous other; the bisexual Catherine Tramell played by Sharon Stone in *Basic Instinct* and the transsexual Jame Gumb, nicknamed 'Buffalo Bill', in *The Silence of the Lambs*. In both films the narrative drive of the hero/heroine to secure his/her place within the symbolically powerful and patriarchal institutions of the police force and the FBI is only resolvable with the outing and death of the other. *The Silence of the Lambs* and *Basic Instinct* are remarkable both for the extremity of their representations of non-heterosexuals as murderous, and also for their literalisation of sub-Freudian explanations for deviant sexuality. In the former, the male villain's kidnapping and murder of a series of women is narratively revealed not as the product of a perverse form of heterosexual activity, but via the homosexual-identified killer's desire to become female. In making a body suit from women's skin, the Jame Gumb character literalises a reading of drag in terms of dressing as a woman. A parallel narrative explanation for the bisexuality of the Stone character is offered in her preferred mode of dispatch: an ice p(r)ick. Her deviant and uncontrolled sexuality is thus accounted for as the result of her misplaced desire to possess the phallus.

In fact in both films the foregrounding of such negative stereotypes might be read as attempting to shift viewers' attention from the collapse of the straight centre from within, as either representations of heroic maleness act unlawfully (*Basic Instinct*) or previously excluded groups such as women enter its sphere (*The Silence of the Lambs*). The assertion of a hypermasculinity allowed to break the rules set for ordinary mortals, literalised in James Bond's licence to kill, has a long history in

Hollywood police thrillers. However its presence in *Basic Instinct* contributed to popular and journalistic readings of the film as Hitchcockian or otherwise retro, somehow too overtly patriarchal for the 1990s.

In *Basic Instinct* it is the addicted, promiscuous and violent white male cop played by Michal Douglas whose sexual fascination with Tramell/Stone leads to the death of his partner. It is only with the supremely violent death of Tramell's female lover Roxy (Leilani Sarelle) that Douglas as Detective Nick Curran can regain his place as cop/lawgiver, reveal the aberrant femininity of the police psychologist (Jeanne Tripplehorn as Dr Beth Garner) and contain the murderous impulse of Stone/Tramell's sexuality. The latter is achieved by the film's display of heterosexual activity initiated by Douglas. It ends with the contented post-coital Stone allowing the ice pick to remain unused beneath the bed. Interestingly, this ending was touted as ambiguous: in addition to the heterosexist reading just outlined, in which the deviant Stone is 'cured' by good straight sex, it keeps open the possibility of Stone's dangerousness. While the latter could still be confined via patriarchal notions of female monstrousness, both of these readings put at stake to some extent the patriarchal power enjoyed by the Douglas character. Endangered by his confidence in his own sexual prowess and his preoccupation with achieving sexual satisfaction, the film also suggests the continuing need for shoring up the heterosexual centre, figured in terms of the necessity for Douglas/Curran to continually perform.

Opening with shots of Jodie Foster's character in physical training, *The Silence of the Lambs* narrates Clarice Starling's entrance and acceptance into the male institution of the FBI. Although her gender implies the fracturing of the heterosexist androcentrism of the thriller genre, with its default heterosexual male hero, it is not represented as a threat. Her femininity is normalised partly via her relationship with boss Jack Crawford (Scott Glenn) as daughterly apprentice, but more strongly against the 'unnatural' and monstrous femininity of the transsexual Jame Gumb. The film constructs a tightly policed essentialised narrative of the relationship of biology and sexuality, basically enforcing the binary penis/heterosexual/good versus masquerade/femininity (i.e. non-biological)/bad. The climactic scene, which after much delay discloses the killer, reveals him as a feminised male, his penis concealed between his legs, adorned with jewellery, absorbed with his own reflection in a mirror. The camera work in this revelation scene, cutting from Gumb's mirror reflection to direct shots of him dancing as a female, displaces the expected male gaze at a sexualised female object. This is disconcerting to straight-identified film audiences, but instead of problematising the power of the heterosexual male gaze, it serves to emphasise the perversity of Gumb's gender-bending. On top of the impact of a murderous kidnapper, the film mobilises a homophobic terror of gender mobility, in which the transsexual uses female skin to displace his male genitalia. The presence of a toy poodle, a familiar accessory to denote gayness, further emphasises the deviance of the character and cannot but identify Gumb's sexual confusion with gayness.

Both *The Silence of the Lambs* and *Basic Instinct* drew negative press and public protest from gay pressure groups such as ACT UP and Queer Nation, focusing on the fact that the only representations of homosexuals allowed by Hollywood were criminalised. This was particularly telling given the contemporaneous release of the adapted *Fried Green Tomatoes* (Jon Avnet, 1991), in which an explicit lesbianism had been removed for the screen. Calls for more balanced and positive representations penetrated the mainstream to some extent, including *Baseline's Encyclopaedia of Film* which expresses reservations about the failure in *The Silence of the Lambs* to separate Buffalo Bill's sexual confusion from his homicidal psychopathy.[8] However, the critical and commercial success of both films (*The Silence of the Lambs* made a clean sweep of the top five Oscars), shows the difficulty in negotiating the social pressures for heterosexual conformity and its attendant homophobia through the stereotype debate.

One response to the problems attendant on engaging with stereotypical constructions of gay and lesbian identity has been the utilisation of an ethnic model as a way of thinking gay and lesbian identity. This move is itself not without risks, as Alan Sinfield among others has warned in his 1996 essay 'Diaspora and hybridity: queer identities and the ethnicity model':

Thinking of lesbians and/or gay men as an ethnic group is a minoritizing move, and it runs counter to the constructed and decentered status of the subject as s/he is apprehended in current theory. Nonetheless, very many lesbians and gay men today feel, intuitively, that the ethnicity model best accounts for them.[9]

Such formulations as this are characteristic of contemporary debates on gay and lesbian identity in positing a dichotomy between on the one hand a politics of rights and egalitarianism, and on the other a thorough-going critique of heterosexist structures. Sinfield understands this dilemma historically as being produced by the construction of gay identity along the lines of ethnicity, post-Stonewall, in order to ground campaigns for gay civil rights. Following Edmund White, Didi Herman, and Cindy Patton, Sinfield stresses the limitations placed upon gay identity and its critique of the *straightgeist* (a term he draws from Nicholson Baker to describe the framework of normative heterosexism, which corresponds to coinages such as compulsory heterosexuality [Adrienne Rich], the heterosexual matrix [Judith Butler], or the straight mind [Monique Wittig]) by its appropriation of the black civil rights model of 'ethnicity-as-rights'.[10] In the essay, Sinfield goes on to arbitrate this dilemma via critical understandings of 1990s gay subcultures and of notions of hybridity as deployed by African American critics. However, placed within the history of representations of gay identity and its criticism, this split between the theory and practice of living, between the desire for a non-essentialist, individuated politics of desire, and the importance of constructing a communal identity that works within the national context, may be neither as new nor as disabling as Sinfield suggests.

The focus on how to recognise gayness either in a positive or negative mode must be understood by reference to the totalising negativity of its status in relation to pre-1970s constructions of American national identity. Like blackness, but more structurally than visibly, gayness stood for the ultimate other, against which normativity could be understood. Russo's work obviously traces this in terms of cinematic images, but this was only part of a general project of uncovering the institutional, legal, medical and biographical discourses and documents which continued to contain and criminalise gay identity and to bolster compulsory heterosexuality. Even understood in isolation from this tradition, ·*The Celluloid Closet* is not simply an uncovering of an oppressive history, but is also a recovering of a subcultural history of gay representation, in ways (camp, drag) that have few parallels in black cultural production. The coded ways in which such forms spoke to and speak to homosexual-identified audiences are made possible primarily by the imbrication of gay sexuality in the construction of normativity; its very importance as totalising negativity. A further crucial term in this subcultural history, the importance of acts of appropriation by gay and lesbian audiences, is also predicated on the invisibility of sexual object choice.

Like *The Celluloid Closet*, works such as Jonathan Ned Katz's *Gay American History*, Jay and Young's *Out of the Closets*, and Faderman's *Odd Girls and Twilight Lovers* show a twofold ambition, arguably borne out of the examples of the black and feminist civil rights movements, of recovering and creating a national and personal narrative of gay American identity.[11] In the 1976 Introduction to *Gay American History*, Katz conceptualised this development in terms of the historicity of gay identities:

> We moved from various forms of self-negation to newfound outrage and action against those lethal conditions. From hiding our sexual and affectional natures, we moved to publically affirm a deep and good part of our being. Starting with a sense of ourselves as characters in a closet drama, the passive victims of a family tragedy, we experienced ourselves as initiators and assertive actors in a movement for social change. We experienced the present as history, ourselves as history-makers. In our lives and in our hearts, we experienced the change from one historical form of homosexuality to another. We experienced homosexuality as historical.[12]

Here and throughout his commentary on the diverse documents assembled in the book, Katz stresses the communal aspect of identity politics. His use of the inclusive 'we', the narratives of coming out of the closet and entering into the public and ideologically circumscribed family domain of American politics and history explicitly situate his work within the growing gay liberation movement. The importance of self-representation both as individual and communal cultural work is stressed, but the impetus for change is not represented as being circumscribed or censored by the preconceptions of the heterosexual mainstream. Thus he goes on:

> I have not been concerned with presenting a 'good image' of homosexuals to heterosexuals – a defensive strategy which limits what Gay people can know of themselves. Thus, those who wish to confirm their stereotypes may find materials here to feed their prejudice.[13]

The refusal to be limited by pre-existing negative stereotypes, to value the historical placing and importance of the individual narrative and to invoke a communal response even in the face of public disavowal (Anita Bryant's Save Our Children movement being only one example of such), has to be seen in the light of the other civil rights movements.

A major importance of the methodologies developed in debate within and alongside the movements of black liberation, feminism, and gay and lesbian politics are that they foreground the constructedness of the default position of straight white patriarchy. Katz's comments demonstrate the possibilities offered by ideas on the relationship of the personal and the political for constructing more progressive identities than closeting, even if this intertwining of the personal and the political produced its own stereotypes. The default position, *once revealed as constructed*, became a potentially transgressive position to take up, one which allowed entrance into further economies of image and desire. It is this which is highlighted by Andrea Weiss in her use of bathroom graffiti as an epigraph to her book on lesbians in the cinema, *Vampires and Violets:*

> When you watch the film *Vertigo* [Hitchcock, 1958], are you Scottie [Jimmy Stewart] wanting Madeleine [Kim Novak], or are you Madeleine wanting Scottie to want you? Or both alternately and simultaneously? In what proportion and what intensities? [14]

One strong move within this critical turn is the authenticating of the critic as knowing partly because of her/his sexual orientation. Following from the work of Rich, Rubin and de Lauretis the establishing of an authentic critical position has often taken the form of the critic outing her or himself. Rather than closing down critical positionality into a singular authentic *ego*, such moves give readerships examples of the personal and historical American identity argued for in the critical texts themselves. The importance of this personalising narrative cannot be dismissed since it offered a connecting example to demonstrate the importance of the complicity of closeted gays and lesbians in reproducing heterosexuality as the default position, and thereby also emphasising the importance of belonging to a shared community. Of course, the privileging of any personal narrative risks reduplicating the essentialising or universalising trends of heterosexual narratives, as was the case in many 1970s critiques from feminist or ethnic positions. However most gay critics follow Katz et al. by situating their identity as a cultural construction. Thus, for example, at the close of her Introduction to *Vampires and Violets*, Weiss asserts that, 'As subjective and personal as my responses to films may seem at times, they are like everything else largely determined by historical and social experience.' [15] But instead of being used to guarantee the authenticity of her readings, this insight frames a sense of the historical limitations of her perspective in comparison with other lesbian readings. Stressing both the critical and the personal elements in her own narrative of lesbian identity, Weiss foregrounds both the communal and the individualistic modes of her groundbreaking work on lesbian film representations. Earlier in the same section she first adopts Russo's strategies for the recovery and production of alternative interpretations, before emphasising the resultant creation of group identities:

> The few lesbian images offered by the cinema were created for heterosexual male viewers, to appeal to male voyeurism about lesbians and to articulate and soothe male sexual anxieties about female autonomy or independence from men. Still, lesbians did go to the movies, and did respond in different ways to these images. From the beginning, lesbians were able to subvert aspects of this powerful visual medium in order to create ways of being lesbian, to construct individual and group lesbian identities.[16]

Obviously the positive results of this critical work have been the pluralising of models of gay and lesbian identity and a widening of debates around such identities by and for gay Americans. However this has not been to the exclusion of the non-gay identified critic. Alexander Doty has written on the possibility of defining a space where the fragmentation of the universalising white straightness would be a liberating arena for all critics, in some measure irrespective of their personal and political orientations. Discussing the use of queer theory he writes 'By using "queer," I want to recapture and reassert a militant sense of difference that views the erotically "marginal" as both (in bell hooks's words) a consciously chosen "site of resistance" and a "location of radical openness and possibility."[17] 'Queer' positioning as developed by Doty implies critical consciousness which is fragmentary and self-divided, allowing for the fragmentation of both individual and community. Such critical consciousnesses are, it seems to us, the most useful in coming to grips with the cross-cut complexity of identity representations that we have been discussing throughout this book. In this context it is interesting to note that Doty references the African American feminist hooks, thus continuing the trend of interaction between the critical spheres of debates over different identity politics.

In the illustrative readings of films that follow we trace the tripartite movement detailed above. This broadly chronological movement might be simplistically schematised as follows. First, a recovery of the history of representations of homosexuality which follows the trajectory of a move from negative to more positive images. This is exemplified by Robert Epstein and Jeffrey Friedman's film of Russo's book, also entitled *The Celluloid Closet* (1995). Second, a positioning of these representations within the national frame of identity politics utilising autobiographical and documentary frames, as exemplified in *The Question of Equality* television series and the films *Tongues Untied* (Marlon Riggs, 1989) and *Stonewall* (Nigel Finch, UK, 1995). Third, the reworking of such representations utilising 'queer' and avant-garde strategies, as in Kalin's *Swoon* (1992) and *Go Fish* (Rose Troche, 1994). We close with an account of Hollywood's response to these developments via a reading of *Philadelphia* (Jonathan Demme, 1993). It should be noted though that these three tendencies are neither separate nor exclusive positions or movements but that an examination of all of them is required to account for the representations of contemporary gay identity on film.

The Celluloid Closet and *The Question of Equality*: Reconstructing gay film history

The film *The Celluloid Closet* is more than an illustration of Russo's book. In its historical and diverse collection of gay representation it gives visual impetus to the book's closing hope and plea:

> [I]t is not gay actors or gay characters but the *idea* of homosexuality for which gays have searched in films, almost always in vain. But the decision to make visible the gay lifestyle is irrevocable, and eventually the movies will have to reflect the diversity of gay existence.[18]

This film is a montage of clips of movies from *The Gay Brothers*, an experimental sound film directed for Thomas Edison in 1895, to the early 1990s, intercut with talking heads discussing this material and the subject of gay representations. The clip from *The Gay Brothers* is repeated at the close of the film and ironically juxtaposed with a shot of Tom Hanks and Antonio Banderas dancing in fancy dress from the party sequence in *Philadelphia*. This elliptical structure visually underscores the one overall message of the film, that gay audiences and gay representations have always been part of the cinema. The film charts a progressive trajectory of the status and the effect of these representations, moving from the overwhelmingly negative stereotypes pre-Stonewall to the more positive contemporary strategic representations.

Following the form of Russo's book, the film traces Hollywood's covert treatment of homosexuality through stereotypes such as the sissy (exemplified from *The Gay Divorcee*: Mark Sandrich, 1934), on to the homosexual/homosocial subplot in reaction to the Hays code, through the pathologised stereotypes of the 1960s and 1970s to the diversity of contemporary representations. The sheer numbers of clips, their generic diversity, the range of stars and character types offer a weighty corrective to the invisibility of homosexuality. The film frames the clips by inter-cutting them with a commentary written by Armistead Maupin and spoken by Lily Tomlin, and comments by a mixture of authoritative talking heads including out critics, writers and actors such as Maupin, Ron Nyswaner, and Richard Dyer and 'straight' screenwriters and actors such as Whoopi Goldberg, Susan Sarandon and Tom Hanks. These innovations open up some contexualising space around the clips which enables them to be critiqued and historicised. Audiences are thereby directed to examine Hollywood as a national institution whose hege-monic hold on image construction can be and has been fractured. *The Celluloid Closet* offers viewers both filmic examples and spoken narrative opinion so as to call attention to the constructedness of representations of homosexuality and their changes through time. It thereby takes up one of the basic elements of Dyer's groundbreaking 1977 work, *Gays and Film*, encouraging the type of active participation in the reading of film representations suggested by Dyer as a means of contesting hege-monic constructions of normativity:

> The establishment of normalcy through social- and stereotypes is one aspect of the habit of ruling groups ... to attempt to fashion the whole of society according to their own world-view, value-sytem, sensibility and ideology ... However, and this cannot be stressed too emphatic-ally, hegemony is an *active* concept – it is something that must be ceaselessly built and rebuilt in the face of both implicit and explicit challenges to it.[19]

In line with resisting the reproduction of hegemony, *The Celluloid Closet* illustrates and critiques the narrative move of Hollywood to re-establish the dominant normativity of heterosexuality. The major means by which this is done is a montage of clips of death scenes from movies as diverse as *Rebel Without a Cause* (Nicholas Ray, 1955), *Rebecca*

(Alfred Hitchcock, 1940) and *The Children's Hour* (William Wyler, 1962), with the voice-over of 'in the last frame characters with questionable sexuality meet with death'. By excerpting these numerous examples from their narrative and symbolic place in the original films, *The Celluloid Closet* challenges the internal and social narratives by which, for homosexuals, untimely death is 'inevitable' or 'natural'.

Of course, as discussed above, this use of negative stereotypes is not just a past historical phenomenon. Examples of deaths or exclusions from the narratives could be used from contemporary films such as *The Silence of the Lambs*, *Basic Instinct*, *Daughters of the Dust* or even *Pretty Woman*, along with the elision or downgrading of lesbian love plots in such adaptations as *The Color Purple* and *Fried Green Tomatoes*. However, the main drive of *The Celluloid Closet* is, as stated above, to trace a positive progressive narrative of gay representation, which culminates with screenwriters and filmmakers breaking the monolith of the heterosexual Hollywood production. It brings Russo's 1981 book up to the 1990s with extended clips from *Philadelphia* and an interview with Tom Hanks, plus an extended montage of very short clips defined as 'new voices'. It concludes elliptically with the Edison film clip voiced over by Maupin:

> Hollywood still runs scared from people who fear the very mention of homosexuality, the very display of it on the screen legitimises the subject. Well of course it does, it shows that homosexuals are human beings. Movies could be making us laugh and cry a lot more if they acknowledged the true diversity of humanity.

Even as Maupin acknowledges the continued existence of a homophobic audience he overlays this with the liberal American plea to universality. An invocation to 'the true diversity of humanity', however positive and well intentioned, does not deal with the ferocity and surveillance of such right-wing groups as Focus on the Family, nor with the way in which, as we argue below, progressive-intentioned representations such as *Philadelphia* might work at the expense of other identity representations. What seems lacking in this plea and from the film *The Celluloid Closet* as a whole is a sense of the larger cultural and political frames of identity representations. While it aids a recovery of the history of representations and explains how gay and straight audiences learned to read with and against these representations individually, it does not situate this in the communal and national debates around gay identity formation. The implication is that 'things can only get better'. The active engagement with heterosexual hegemony encouraged by Dyer is missing, as is a sense of the instrumental and symbolic uses to which homosexual representations have been put. As we have suggested, it is important to couple the history of representations to a full sense of the complexities of parallel political movements and debates. The trajectory described in *The Celluloid Closet* film, from exclusion from the mainstream to a state of undifferentiated diversity, does not take on the historical and contemporary plurality of gay identity politics and their representations.

In fact the sight and sounds of the gay civil rights movements are strangely absent both from voice-overs and the film's images. In order to introduce material from *The Boys in the Band* (William Friedkin, 1970), very brief footage of a gay liberation march, raids on gay bars and the continuing treatment of homosexuality as a psychiatric disease are montaged together without contextualising comment. Moreover, the power of these images is reduced by the film's location of *The Boys in the Band* in the progressive trajectory described above, in contrast to the more problematical status accorded to it in Russo's book. Later, further brief footage is shown of a Gay Liberation Front protest at showings of *Cruising* (William Friedkin, 1980). This downplaying of the effect of such movements strangely depoliticises the film, resolving prematurely the tensions of who or what is or can be represented as gay and American. In its desire to make visible homosexuality, *The Celluloid Closet* homogenises it in terms of the totalising structure of the heterosexual symbolic economy. Ironically, therefore, just as it offers itself as a tool to fracture dominant heterosexist constructions of the hero and of identity in general, the film's marginalisation of the communal narrative reinforces just such constructions.

The reasons for the exclusion of these narratives are explained by their status as communal and explicitly political. More difficult to assimilate into dominant cultural models of inclusiveness, they appear as less saleable to a Hollywood aiming to maximise rather than to fragment its audience. With respect to models of national identity, emphasis on such narratives represents difference as unrecuperable by liberal 'melting pot' notions of diversity. Hollywood is therefore always more at ease in producing films such as *The Birdcage* (Mike Nichols, 1996), which while they construct sexuality in terms of sexual object-choice continue to exclude a sense of histories of repression, contestation and liberation.

However, alternative representations can be found which add to and complement *The Celluloid Closet* film. Documentary series such as *The Question of Equality* and autobiographical documentary forms offer a parallel narrative of the formation of gay American identity. Such sources broaden and contextualise mainstream representations. They follow the critical turn of interpolating together the personal and the political that we have described in the work of gay and lesbian critics, and they have in turn, as we will show, shaped the form and content of mainstream and independent representations of gayness.

The Question of Equality, screened in the UK as *Over the Rainbow*, can be seen to follow Katz and Dyer in documenting and countering heterosexist constructions of gay identity. In its use of historical and contemporary news and other video footage with talking heads and further oral accounts spliced in, it echoes the format of *The Celluloid Closet*. However, *The Question of Equality* eschews a linear progressive narrative and focuses on the plurality of gay identity, representing the conflicting movements within the gay community even as they are under attack by anti-gay groups such as Pat Robertson's Christian Coalition. As David Meieran writes in the Preface to the companion book to the series:

> Ultimately, the absence of a consensus on broader issues helped us to realise that this documentary could neither presume lesbian and gay harmony, nor shy away from the conflicts and contradictions that have marked the movement, past and present. The questions that needed to be asked about lesbian and gay equality concern internal conflicts every bit as much as they do the external challenges of people who would like us to return to the closet.[20]

The combination in *The Question of Equality* of visual representation and oral history situates and exemplifies the civil rights struggle, offering a plurality of representations of gay identity to its audience. These are not hierarchised by their approximation to mainstream preconceptions. Hence in the first episode the post-Stonewall emergence of gay groups is shown in its fractured actuality as the splitting of the Gay Liberation Front into groups such as the Gay Activists Alliance and the Lesbian Liberation Front. This narrative is overlaid with images of the first gay protest marches and first-hand accounts of the Stonewall riots by such as Sylvia (Ray) Rivera, co-founder of STAR (Street Transvestite Action Revolutionaries). As with *The Celluloid Closet* film, the numbers of images and oral histories make visible a history of homosexuality, but here this history is plural and openly contests both the hegemony of the heterosexual gaze and what could be described as the emerging monolith of white homosexual identity. By showing such different identities as those represented by Rivera, a Latino/a male-to-female transvestite and Jewelle Gomez, an African American lesbian, alongside white gay man Bob Kohler, and by tracing their differing experiences of the post-Stonewall gay experience, the documentary refuses to homogenise their identity in an assimilable form. Thus, for example, Rivera's recollections of the Stonewall uprising are prefaced by a sense of the differences between gay identities:

> Drag queens and effeminate men were never in a closet. What kills me as a drag queen is that I can go into a gay bar and listen to these so-called macho gay men, 'Oh, Mary this, and Miss Thing that.' But as soon as I walk into a bar, they know where I'm coming from, and right away I'm shunted aside.[21]

The descriptions of Gomez and Kohler constitute further discrete historical perspectives which overlap and clash rather than producing a rounded kaleidoscopic narrative. For Gomez, writing in essay form by way of introducing the first-hand accounts in the book of the documentary,

> The significance of these demonstrations may have been more personal than public. Stepping from the closet out into the open air gave each person walking the picket line a chance to see herself within the context of her country, not just her lover or other bar patrons. Each picketer was also able to see others like himself; not imagined shadows in a fantasy book or back room, but adult men walking on a public street.[22]

Kohler's account is, like Rivera's, taken verbatim from the documentary and presented in one of the book's 'In their own words' sections:

> Everything happened all at once, which it does in a riot or disaster. I had my dog with me, so I was worried about him and about one of the street kids. I was trying to keep them both out of harm's way. It just started with bottles, windows breaking, trashcans, fires, then the fire engines ... The police were totally at the mercy of the crowd.[23]

In spite of their inconsistencies these accounts illustrate the importance of communal action and its representation as against the films of the period which were still representing homosexuality as either an isolated, affectionless and self-destructive life choice, as in *Midnight Cowboy* (John Schlesinger, 1969); as an emergent threat to mainstream heterosexuality, and therefore to be violently expunged (John Boorman's *Deliverance*, 1972) and/or as degenerate, as in *Scarecrow* (Jerry Schatzberg, 1973).

Even the breakthrough 1970 film *The Boys in the Band*, described by Russo as 'the first Hollywood film in which all the principal characters are homosexual', makes no reference to public, national and communal narratives.[24] The first film to represent a group of male homosexuals does so through the narrative device of a birthday party, an enclosed private space in Manhattan. Both Russo and Dyer focus critiques of *The Boys in the Band* by reference to its use, as Russo put it, 'of easily acceptable stereotypes who ... spend an evening savaging each other and their way of life.'[25] Dyer goes on, 'By setting it in a private home and excluding non-gay characters (except Alan) and women, the drama is located in individual personalities, personal strengths and weaknesses.'[26] The placing of stereotypical characters in a privatised space, isolated from histories of resistance and from a wider gay community determines that any possible communal identity and impetus against mainstream oppression is excluded or internalised as self-hatred. The symbolic economy of *The Boys in the Band* reproduces constructions of difference as negative and disempowering. The best that can be hoped for then is to internalise and in some sense come to terms with the (at best) unfortunate condition of homosexuality. This state of affairs is made explicit in perhaps the film's most plangent and melodramatic speech, where the stereotypical Harold (Leonard Frey) rounds on the more closeted Michael (Kenneth Nelson):

> You are a sad and pathetic man, Michael. You are a homosexual, and you don't want to be, but there's nothing you can do to change it. Not all your prayers to your God. Not all the analysis your money can buy in the years you have left to live. You may one day be able to know a heterosexual life. If you want it desperately enough. If you pursue it with the fervour with which you annihilate. But you will always be homosexual as well, Michael. Always. Until the day you die.[27]

Aside from *The Question of Equality*, few USA productions have explicitly set out to correct these representations. Before going on to discuss independent and arguably avant-gardist films by Marlon Riggs and Tom Kalin, we will concentrate on explicit attempts to represent national narratives of gay identity in Finch's *Stonewall* and in *Looking for Langston* (Isaac Julien, UK, 1988). That both of these directors are originally British, and that the films were largely funded from outside the USA can be read in two ways. It illustrates the global importance of gay movements in America through their transatlantic influence. Finch's film implies that the symbolic importance of Stonewall is not bounded by national imperatives, while Julien explores the importance of the relationship between black and gay identity through the representation of the gay Harlem Renaissance poet Langston Hughes. It also points out the lack of interest Hollywood has had in projects such as these. Representations which are overtly political or which radically critique stereotypes have tended to be produced much more readily in the independent or public broadcasting arena. Made in the USA, *Stonewall* was funded by the BBC.

Stonewall's romances of resistance

Stonewall contextualises the riot outside the Stonewall Inn in late June 1969. The film is framed at beginning and end as the reminiscence of one of its central characters, drag queen LaMiranda, played by Guillermo Diaz. At the opening of the film, LaMiranda/Diaz announces to the camera, 'There are as many Stonewall stories as there are gay queens in New York. This is my Stonewall legend.' As this quotation suggests, while this framing device recognises the historic/mythic status of the riot, the film does not simply privilege this one perspective. Unlike in *The Boys in the Band*, the plurality of late 1960s urban gay life is represented in both public and private spheres. The film depicts drag queens of different ethnicities, a closeted Italian gangster, and white female and male gay activists on a broad spectrum of gay life. Equal focus is given to both the homophile political movements such as the Mattachine Society and the Daughters of Bilitis, and the street and subculture of the bars in Greenwich Village. The film shows the separation of these two groups in terms of attitudes to gay identity while at the same time showing a number of romance narratives which lead to interaction between the groups. Thus, as with the relevant episode of *The Question of Equality* and *Over the Rainbow*'s deployment of quotations from Rivera, Gomez and Kohler, the narrative of the events is not dominated from one viewpoint, nor is there any attempt to construct a privileged heterosexual perspective.

Stonewall uses a number of devices both to historically situate itself and to signal its difference from mainstream narratives. It opens with historical black and white footage of the riot intercut with reconstructions of it and with recollections by participants such as Bob Kohler filmed as talking heads. This situates the following film as gay history, that is as part of a project to reclaim representation, and might be likened to the similar use of historical sources in *Malcolm X* and in *Glory*. The main body of the film, though it utilises a romance structure, also stages the fracturing of realist conventions when from time to time the narrative is interrupted by versions of the musical number. These numbers take the form of the drag queens miming to camera songs by girl groups such as the Shangri-Las and the Shirelles, thus both breaking the frame and ironising the heterosexual narratives of songs like '(Remember) Walking on the Sand'. Therefore, while it might be aligned to projects such as *Glory* in its retelling of history and its reshaping of stereotypes, *Stonewall* attempts to separate itself from the hegemonic heterosexual aesthetics of mainstream filmmaking.

The main narrative concerns Latino/a drag queen LaMiranda and Matty Dean (Frederick Weller), a white middle-class Bostonian who has travelled to New York to be part of the social and political scene. These two characters are recognisable stereotypes who can be read as symbolic of the two main groupings of gay identity in the film, the white homophile groups and the subculture of drag queens and other street people. Hence one segment of gay identity is demonstrated in the hyperfemininity of the drag queen who, rejected by his/her family, belongs to a social grouping of other queens. The group of drag queens is mutually supportive but lacks political consciousness and organisation. This is complemented by the blond, clean-cut college boy radical from Boston who chooses to come out to his family and wants, he says, to change America. It is through the developing romance between these two and among subsidiary characters, culminating in their participation in the riot, that the film frames the eruption of the gay civil rights movement.

This and the other narratives of romance, affection and sexuality function in several ways in the film. It could be argued that the use of the romance narrative with its overwhelmingly heterosexual connotations and conformity to American family values represents a normative construction of gay identity, that is, that gays desire to be like heterosexuals. Such a reading encodes the film as advocating an assimilationist stance like that of the homophile groups it represents, who rule that all participants on the march in Philadelphia wear conservative clothes and haircuts and biological gender-specific clothing. However, this reading is strategically undercut in *Stonewall*. For a start, the film offers audiences a variety of possible full relationships rather than privileging the potentially straight-identified romance between LaMiranda and Matty Dean. Just as importantly, appearance and life narratives are both carefully represented as being markers of identity formation and as functioning to keep sexual identity visible and empowered. Hence the self-imposed conformity to dress codes on the official protests is recontextualised when a police raid on the Stonewall bar invokes the legal requirement for three gender-specific pieces of clothing. The film is here producing a history of the political uses of clothing which allows both conforming and dragging up to be read as political. Thus the homophile groups' adoption of straight dress codes can be understood not as inadvertently buying into a paradigm of heterosexuality, but as a condition enforced by the hysterical nature of the heterosexual mainstream. Conversely, the ironic use of songs intended to fuel feelings of heterosexual romance in young American girls shows how mainstream culture can be and was appropriated. The film emphases this relationship by intercutting shots of the homophiles preparing for the march and the drag queen chorus miming the Shangri-Las' 'Sophisticated Boom Boom'.

All of the romance narratives in *Stonewall* function to underline the 'message' of the film, that the personal was and always has been political for gay Americans. The relationship of LaMiranda and Matty is offered to the audience as constituting a personal and political viewpoint to understand Stonewall. It humanises the larger political frame but does not privilege one form of gay identity; nor does it deny the problematics of gay and ethnic identity politics. As critics have noticed, there has been a tendency by both gay and straight groups to downplay the involvement of the drag queens and street people in the riot. Discussing gay self-censorship, Jewelle Gomez writes that

In 1969 [censorious aspects of ourselves] let some of us ignore the

Stonewall riots, or some of us even to condemn them. Because of all of those boys with no eyebrows. The specifics of exactly who was there have varied in the telling, but it is clear that this was not an Ivy League crew. They were not neatly starched students but rather hustlers and street people living a rough life – not one that we wanted to see on television.[28]

While the romance of LaMiranda and Matty overcomes several difficulties, many of the other sexual relationships foregrounded in the film end unsatisfactorily or tragically. The film's depiction of the relationships between Ethan (Brendan Corbalis) and Matty, and most strikingly Vinnie (Bruce MacVittie), the closeted owner of the bar, and drag queen Bustonia (Duane Boutté), shows up the romance allowed by mainstream society as a cultural construction whose rules and codes exclude same-sex participation. Hence the significance of Vinnie asking Bustonia to have a sex change so that he can be 'an ordinary man' and go out in public with him/her. Vinnie's bloody suicide after one ludic day *out* strategically shocks the audience. The only possible explanation is that he has killed himself because of the pressure to conform. By juxtaposing the celebratory and often funny representation of Vinnie and Bustonia's public deployment of gayness with Vinnie's suicide, the film avoids reproducing the stereotype of the self-hating homosexual. Instead, the tragedy reinforces a sense of the destructive effects of the prescriptions of heterosexual codes and should propel audiences to seek change. By way of a somewhat lighter comparison, *Stonewall* offers a tea dance scene on Fire Island. Here gay men can only dance if a mixed male and female couple are dancing, and even then their self-policing does not allow touching. Such scenes point up the ludicrousness of the notion that coupling in a structure, whether fictive or real, could only be done by heterosexuals.

Though LaMiranda is not actually living on the street she does work on it. *Stonewall* offers both hustlers and students as heroes and positive representations. It also foregrounds ethnicity. The contrast between on the one side the white homophile societies and the white gay scene in Fire Island, and on the other side the ethnically mixed community centred on the street and the bar, is continuously played up. Latino/a and African American drag queens are represented as sassy and powerful, and the most violent action of the film, aside from the riot, concerns LaMiranda's refusal to wash off his/her makeup. On one level this could be seen to be playing to the negative stereotypes of the exotic and lively ethnic or the gay sambo. But, as Gomez implies, it is important to recognise the actual composition of the Stonewall rioters, and their double and triple marginalisation in mainstream, gay and ethnic contexts.

In this sense, *Stonewall* has much in common with films such as Isaac Julien's *Looking for Langston* (1988) and Marlon Riggs's *Tongues Untied* (1989). All three films register the crucial importance of representations of ethnicity and gayness, given the much discussed homophobia in the mainstream black civil rights movement. Its persistence is demonstrated by the reported remarks of Dr Molefi Kete Asante, director of Temple University's black studies programme, that 'homosexuality is a deviation from Afrocentric thought, because it makes the person evaluate his own physical needs above the teachings of national consciousness.' [29] Against such formulations and attempts to fix positive images of blackness or gayness the films of Finch, Julien and Riggs seek to record and to perpetuate the complexity of gay identity.

Julien's attempt to reveal Langston Hughes as a gay, black poet of the Harlem Renaissance has become a locus for debate concerning black identity on both sides of the Atlantic. The critical focus has been to stress its importance in retrieving a suppressed past – gay black identity – while locating the reasons for its suppression in the heterosexual mainstreams of both black and white culture. Thus for Henry Louis Gates, Jr.:

[A] film like *Looking for Langston* is able to respond to the hurtfully exclusionary obsessions of the black nationalist moment, and our own cultural moment as well, by constructing a counter-history in which desire and mourning and identity can interact in their full complexity, but in a way that registers the violence of history. [30]

While it is stylistically less innovative than *Looking for Langston*, *Stonewall* engages in similar cultural work.

The film ends with LaMiranda again talking to camera. She asserts 'We deal in dreams. We're American as apple pie.' This closing comment enacts the film's strategies of calling attention to its own fictive status while also soliciting audience engagement. It is a dream, but 'we' are part of it. The interpolation of the audience via the tag of national identity is important in connecting audience members personally through their stories to the communal movement. LaMiranda's personal story is one of politics, his/her identity as an ethnic gay. Such interpolation of the personal and the historical is, as we have seen, a recurring motif in the critical and the filmic work under examination here.

Tongues Untied and national narratives of black and gay identity

Like that of Julien and Finch, the work of the late African American gay filmmaker Marlon Riggs is structured by the production of filmic histories in relation to gay and ethnic/racial communities. The address of Riggs's work has been more autobiographical, using personal history to connect debates over sexual and ethnic identity with the need to counter both white and black American homophobia. In *Over the Rainbow* Riggs is quoted as follows:

> So much of being black in this country and being gay in this country is effacing who you are, so that you can assimilate, so that you can be a part of the larger culture, and nobody will notice you, so that you can be invisible, because once you become visible ... that becomes a problem in other people's minds.[31]

Riggs's 1989 film *Tongues Untied* can be read as furthering and contemporising the agenda of *Looking for Langston*. The two films are cross-referenced by their use of Essex Hemphill's poetry. Riggs also links the projects in an early sequence of a man phoning a sex line, while visible onscreen is a still from *Looking for Langston* showing two naked and embracing African American men. It is shot in both colour and black and white and mixes Riggs's own first-person narration with poetry, dance, and footage of homophobic Christian and nationalist speeches, and gay and civil rights marches in New York and Selma. *Tongues Untied* is non-linear and formally confrontational, utilising documentary techniques alongside atmospheric black and white segments illustrating Hemphill's poetry. Riggs's film thereby contrasts markedly with the realist narratives of the directors associated with the 'new jack cinema', whose work has been critiqued for perpetuating the negative stereotyping of black femininity and using the realist form to construct a representation of nationalistic, macho, heterosexist black masculinity as the authentic and only real black masculinity. For Valerie

Smith, 'the techniques and narratives of these films ... conceal their status as mediations and suggest that they occupy an intimate, if not contiguous, relation to an externally verifiable reality.'[32] In the reality represented by these films no gay black identity is possible. It is this absence and silence that Riggs counters both in form and content. Smith situates Riggs in a tradition of filmmakers whose project is to represent the invisible. It is this which contextualises the radicality of its form:

> The film shows how homophobia among black and non-black heterosexuals, racism among white gays, and the AIDS epidemic have combined to silence the voices of black gay men. The multiplicity of voices in the film both illustrates the diversity of gay black male perspectives and dramatises the insistence of the forces that seek to obliterate them. Visuals and soundtrack alike in this film deconstruct viewers' expectations of linear narrative and the authoritative voice-over, thereby challenging monolithic notions of black gay identity.[33]

This is an acute description of *Tongues Untied*, in which segments featuring a black drag queen are juxtaposed with a gay black man on the streets of San Francisco, with street vogueing and choreographed dance pieces; Billie Holiday singing is intercut with oral testimony such as 'in this great gay mecca I was an invisible man. I was an alien. I was a nigger still.' The challenge to monolithic identity constructions is maintained throughout the film, but there is also a narrative progression which helps to construct a strong viewing position. *Tongues Untied* is engaged in both deconstructive and constructive cultural work, moving to replace monoliths not with disabling fragmentation but with alternative and communal notions of identity. As we will argue, the response solicited by the film is a move out of the closet and onto the streets, a politicisation of black gay identity paralleling the black civil rights movements of the 1960s.

What powers this narrative progression is the call to end the silence about black gay identity, which is repeated throughout the differing segments, challenging the viewer to respond. The following quotations from different parts of the film illustrate its trajectory:

> Silence is my cloak
> By silence you are complicit
> Silence is my sword

It [silence] cuts both ways
Now I speak my burden is lifted.

This movement culminates with the slogan 'Black men loving black men is *the* revolutionary act' which appears in the form of intertitles. The need for this movement is underlined by the use of such visual representations as footage of a homophobic routine from an Eddie Murphy concert, and headshots of homophobic rants by a black preacher and a black nationalist. Such images not only explain the silence but demonstrate the need to answer such negative constructions of homosexuality.

On a basic level, Riggs uses an autobiographical narrative to illustrate how to be part of this revolution, via representing his difficulty in negotiating his initial desire for white gays rather than black, and his subsequent articulation and acting on his desire for black gays. Outside the film Riggs has foregrounded the importance of personal experience in the construction of a communal identity, describing himself in interview as 'a transition, a link', and as 'speaking directly to the experiences of people trying to find identity and find community when the world was telling them that they had none'.[34]

With more limited scope *Tongues Untied* offers another way into this 'revolution' via appropriating heterosexual cultural forms. One segment features a parody of such R&B groups as the Four Tops, in which a white-suited group sing a chorus of 'Hey boy come out tonight'. Like the later drag queen chorus in *Stonewall*, this reverses the heterosexual bias of the original, while the dual reference of 'out' to socialising and leaving the closet links the personal and the political.

The narrative drive of these individual instances is replicated in the overall structure of the film, which moves from representations of individual stories in domestic space, through images of the predominantly white Castro area of San Francisco and street scenes of vogueing in New York at night, to gay rights marches in New York in daylight. This trajectory thus represents both an individual narrative of coming out and also the pattern of gay history. The move is from the closeted gay individual to a social grouping which is actually and symbolically contained in the dark on the streets or in bars, to the open civil rights protest in daylight signalling the end of silence. Riggs emphasises the national and political frame of gay identity and the specificity of blackness through ending the film by fading back and forth between footage of contemporary gay civil rights marches into images of King and the Selma marches. Thus he positions gay and black rights visually and ideologically on the same historical continuum.

That the strategies of *Tongues Untied* challenge mainstream heterosexual values is apparent from the use of selective segments by proposive Republican presidential candidate Pat Buchanan in the Georgia presidential primary. The segment representing white gay men on Castro Street with leather chaps and bare bottoms was used by Buchanan to argue that George Bush supported obscene material through the funding of the NEA (National Endowment for the Arts). As Mab Segrest has pointed out, this appropriation of Riggs's work was one result of backlash strategies developed by the religious right over a long period of time, and which had one sort of culmination in the making and distribution in the late 1980s of *The Gay Agenda*.[35] Distributed widely and free of charge to Christian and education institutions, politicians and the military, this video used footage of gay civil rights marches in San Francisco, among other images, to rework negative and criminal gay stereotypes as emblematic of all lesbian and gay activity. It is against such representations and the hard right agenda of US-wide attempts to bring in homophobic legislation that the work of Riggs and others must be read.[36] Discussion of Riggs's formal innovations must therefore take place in the context of creating alternative identities, histories and communal movements, rather than via notions of avant-gardism.

Swoon: murdering stereotypes

The result of Riggs's contestation of the double oppression of black/gay identity might however be seen as problematic for its exclusion of white gay identity or lesbian representations. In addition, a focus on and belief in the efficacy of the particular positive images constructed in *Tongues Untied* is not universal. A new grouping of filmmakers has emerged defined rather vaguely as 'new voices' by *The Celluloid Closet* film and as 'new queer cinema' by such critics as B. Ruby Rich. Filmmakers such as Tom Kalin, Gregg Araki and Rose Troche can be read as refusing to be contained by either the positive images debate, mainstream aesthetics, or desire for the realist albeit alternative histories of the sort discussed above. As Rich put it in 1992:

Of course, the new queer films and videos aren't all the same, and don't share a single aesthetic vocabulary or strategy or concern. Yet they are nonetheless united by a common style. Call it 'Homo Pomo': there are traces in all of them of appropriation and pastiche, irony, as well as a reworking of history with social constructionism very much in mind. Definitively breaking with older humanist approaches and the films and tapes that accompanied identity politics, these works are irreverent, energetic, alternately minimalist and excessive.[37]

Rich typifies the critical reception of new queer cinema in stressing the oppositional style/aesthetics of the films, and focusing on the ways in which they utilise avant-garde techniques to construct representations and objects of desire which are emphatically not politically correct. Hence, in *Swoon* (Tom Kalin, 1992) and Gregg Araki's *The Living End* (1992) respectively, the pre-eminent examples of gay identity are child murderers and HIV positive criminals on the run. There is no attempt by either director to court an audience expecting either the dominant heterosexual gaze or a normative gay desire. Asked about the importance of positive representation in relation to *Swoon*, Kalin answers:

It has its place because it represents many lives, but it doesn't represent my desires. I'm not going to make myself a slave to a political programme that doesn't benefit me. I think the solution is to make more images rather than less: if someone hates this movie, they should make something that counters it.[38]

It could be argued that this is a risky strategy which potentially adds to the dissemination of negative representations in material such as *The Gay Agenda*. However, despite Kalin's lack of interest in producing positive images, his work and *Swoon* in particular can still be situated in relation to the trajectory of productions of gay histories and identities under discussion. Directors such as Kalin are still working to reconstruct and define American gay identity. The films of Kalin and Araki challenge audiences to rethink identity constructions through a complex negotiation of problematic desires and discourses of representation. Just as much as Riggs or Finch these new voices want to make visible gay identity – murderous or not.

Swoon is an obvious example of this kind of cultural work as it represents the case of the 1920s child-murderers Leopold and Loeb by confronting the audience with erotic sexual images, intercut with 1920s footage and accurate courtroom scenes with tableaux of actors, breaking the frame of the film in the opening shot. It eschews realism and as the trailer line for the film announced, 'Puts the Homo back in Homicide'. As we argued above with respect to *The Silence of the Lambs* and *Basic Instinct*, it may well be thought that there is quite enough homo in homicide already, and that the perpetuation of this negative stereotyping by Demme and Verhoeven needs no assistance from an out gay film-maker. However, we would argue that, far from replacing negative treatments with positive ones, Kalin's project is best understood as an examination of the historical and contemporary mainsteam discourses that allow the perpetuation of the positive/negative binary. The film represents the effects on homosexual identity that such discourses produce. This allows the film's formal innovations to be read in terms of historical analysis. As Amy Taubin has argued,

> Kalin makes a pretty clear case for the process by which internalised homophobia and anti-semitism are transformed into sado-masochistic fantasies and a fascination with criminality. The first half of the film unabashedly identifies with Leopold, with his equation of glamour and deviance. If his homosexuality places him outside the law, it's also his connection to Chicago's underworld.[39]

Swoon thus exposes the interrelation of allowable narratives of masculinity, the hypocrisy of the 1920s and subsequent glamorising of gangster criminality so long as it is firmly heterosexual.

In the second half of the film the representation of the trial and imprisonment of Leopold and Loeb shows the hysterical reaction of legal, medical and other discourses of mainstream society. *Swoon* thereby forces audiences to position themselves with these homophobic discourses if they wish for a narrative resolution of punishment. This position is made extremely uncomfortable, and requires that audiences align themselves with the Ku Klux Klan's reported threat that 'If the court don't get them we will.' The type of confrontational imaging made here could be identified with a personal perversity, and Kalin's remark quoted above could be used to support such a reading. However, this is to negate Kalin's emphasis on the historical discourses around homosexuality, visible elsewhere in his controversial work in showing the lack of adequate governmental action about AIDS prevention in his position as associate producer at AIDS Films, and his description of the genesis of *Swoon*:

I applied [for funding] with a treatment called *Intolerance*, written with Hilton Als. I was originally going to do an ambitious piece that took the structure of D. W. Griffith's story and produced a reading of lesbian and gay marginalization in twentieth-century culture by taking specific historical episodes – the Leopold/Loeb case was going to be just one – and attempting to link them up: how what happened in 1913 related to 1924, related to the mid 50s, related to now.[40]

The primary mechanisms of marginalisation exposed in Kalin's film are discourses of sexuality, criminality and ethnicity. *Swoon* works by drawing attention to these discourses and then undercutting them by juxtaposition with each other and with conflicting representations. In the courtroom scenes, for example, Kalin uses original transcripts of the trial and examples of press reporting of the case to show the homophobia of 1920s America. When evidence of their sexual practices is being given by the police and an alienist, the audience hears descriptions of it in their fully unerotic and voyeuristic terms, such as 'Nathan was to have the privilege of inserting his penis between Dick's legs three times a month if their criminal action continued.' This contrasts with the earlier sensual and erotic images of their lovemaking. At this point the judge orders the court cleared of women, even the court stenographer, stating that the evidence is not fit for their ears. Thus in making explicit the way in which homosexuality was seen as an aberrant taboo, Kalin links the benevolent misogyny of 1920s America with the suppression of homosexuality.

This exposure of the discourses surrounding homosexuality culminates in the District Attorney's summing-up speech, which calls for death by hanging 'In the name of the State of Illinois, in the name of fatherhood, in the name of womanhood, for the sake of the children'. The DA is clearly seen here to be marshalling the forces of national and personal narratives of heterosexuality on the side of moral probity and therefore constructing any alternative identity as un-American and unnatural. The status of this presumption is immediately questioned by the film's cutting to a number of still shots of heads presented as examples of scientific phrenology. These stills exemplify both contemporary scientific approaches to criminality and the medical and legal discourses which labelled homosexuality as a perversion and an illness. The heads have captions which heavily ironise such discourses and demonstrate their dependence on the prevailing homophobic morality. The captions, complete with arrows to certain facial features, include the following: 'Feminine nature shows in nose'; 'Pineal gland: secretive, untruthful'; 'Higher moral sense'; 'Thyroid gland: great love of sex'; 'Sensuous lips – implies lewdness'; 'Excessive self esteem'. Comic as these are made to seem, one need only to look at Katz's *Gay American History* to see their historical power. In one sense, then, *Swoon* can be read as a history lesson on the repressive discourses of sexuality. However, the film refuses to allow the stable audience position which might passively absorb such information. The effect of this material at this point is to unsettle audience members, who are left to question how to know that someone is criminal and/or gay if scientific methods are suspect.

This unsettling effect is enhanced a little later in the film by its juxtaposition of representations of Dick's death in prison with radio reportage of the same event. The film clearly shows that Dick is killed by James Day, a white fellow prisoner who it is suggested was attempting to rape him. Subsequently, though, a radio report is shown which describes the killer as a negro protecting himself against sexual advances by Dick, whose 'slobbering lips' outraged him into protecting his manly black heterosexuality. The changes in ethnicity and power position between the event as shown on screen and the radio reportage again makes the audience question the basis of their conceptions. If all of these modes of representation, legal, medical, journalistic, are unreliable, who or what can be relied upon?

Neither does the film offer its own representation of the murder as definitive. As well as problematising historical and material discourses *Swoon* also examines the function of visual representations in constructing realities. This is made explicit from the first frames of the film, which seem to be a realist representation of an outdoor 1920s scene. As the camera draws back, what has been presumed to be actual sky peels back across the frame to reveal the 'real' sky and subsequently we see the whole apparatus of cinematic production, camera lights and technicians in 1990s clothing. Clearly Kalin is signalling the artificiality of (his) film. As with the devices mentioned above, *Swoon* continually prods its audience into an awareness of the constructedness of what it is watching, and this extends both to its form and its re-evaluation of available images of gay identity. Such self-reflexivity at the level of form and the imaging of identity is further emphasised by an understanding of the film's historical significance. Though *Swoon* is in effect the third filmic interpretation of the Leopold/Loeb story after Hitchcock's *Rope*

(1948) and *Compulsion* (Richard Fleischer, 1959), it is widely recognised as the first to explicity represent the homosexual relationship of the two.

To sum up then, though Kalin's strategy can be seen as dangerous given the right wing backlash, it is also undoubtedly disruptive of mainstream structures for the consumption of discourse in general and for audience's consumption of images in particular. However, the end result of this disruption remains problematic. Amy Taubin, for example, has pointed to *Swoon*, *The Living End* and *Tongues Untied* as being 'heedlessly misogynistic'. She sees the androcentrism of these films as positioning them closer to Hollywood traditions than to counter-cultural cinema:

> In fact, this queer cinema has more in common with the current crop of male violence films ... than it does with any feminist cinema. Like Tarantino and [Nick] Gomez, Araki and Kalin are also the sons of Scorsese, whose films define and critique masculinity through violence but also make Robert De Niro a homoerotic object of desire.[41]

It would seem that even the radicality of such queer representations as Kalin's remain reliant on the othering or exclusion of a structural other, here a feminist identity. As we have been arguing throughout this book, in negotiating the competing elements of contemporary American identity, even though the terms and content of the centred, default or mainstream position may be changing and less stable than previously, the structuring paradigm is usually still one of centre and margin. In this case it seems that gay identity is foregrounded and represented at the expense of a feminist identity. Of course, a similar critique could be made of films such as Rose Troche's *Go Fish* (1994) whose representations of homosexuality are all lesbian, but this would be to overly simplify Taubin's position and our own. It is not that *Swoon* and *The Living End* lack representations of females, positive or negative. It is that the progressive challenging of mainstream discourses in these films depends upon suppressing the feminist critique of constructions of maleness (straight or gay) which naturalise the relationship between masculinity and violence. While *Go Fish* does deconstruct mainstream discourses of heterosexuality in ways similar to *Swoon*, it arguably does not replace them with discourses which replicate the disempowering structure of heterosexuality.

Go Fish: lesbian romances of resistance

As the work of Weiss and Russo discussed above shows, there is a history of mainstream representations of lesbian identity, albeit a negative one. Weiss stresses the importance of the civil rights movements in challenging this negativity:

> The 1970s and 80s women's and gay liberation movements can be seen to have had a positive impact on the dominant cinema, through the appearance of 'attractive' lesbian characters in such films as *Silkwood* [Mike Nichols, 1983] or *Personal Best* [Robert Towne, 1982], but a closer look at these films reveals that their lesbian relationships are still mapped onto, and seen as poor imitations of, non-lesbian models: mother/daughter has merely replaced male/female.[42]

The continuing focus on the problematics of masculinity has resulted in a comparable lack of widely disseminated representations of lesbian identity. Even when there is a mainstream representation that is not reliant on the co-opting of the type described by Weiss it is usually marginal in screen time. Portrayals such as the lesbian cop played by Laurie Metcalf in *Internal Affairs* (Mike Figgis, 1990), who is out and respected by co-workers and is shown to be good at her job, obviously constitute a progressive move away from the stereotypical villains and vampiric stereotypes associated with lesbianism. Yet, as Cindy Patton has argued, this character is only integral to the plot in so far as she grounds heterosexuality. For Patton, *Internal Affairs* 'depended on gay and lesbian theme films to ensure that the intense relationship between the two male protagonists could distance itself from the unselfconscious homoeroticism of earlier cop films'.[43] Therefore, however positive some contemporary representations may be judged, and they should be balanced against such negative representations as those in *Basic Instinct*, they remain visually and ideologically on the periphery. As collections such as *Queer Looks* and *Out in Culture* have stressed, much cultural work has been done in constructing and producing representations of lesbian identity, but these are underfunded, on a small scale, on video, or are documentary/avant-garde in form and therefore have not gained a wide or national status.[44] One of the few films which has broken into the mainstream but also critiques the negative or normative stereotypes of lesbian representation is *Go Fish*.

Troche's film eschews the normalising heterosexist frames used in

Silkwood and *Personal Best*, representing a group of out twenty- and thirty-something lesbians in a private and public world which is not reliant on the approbation of mainstream society. Shot in black and white it represents the developing romance between two characters, Max (Guinevere Turner) and Ely (V. S. Brodie). This narrative is intercut with talking heads shots of their friends commenting on the relationship, and with sequences which explore internal gay oppression and the dominance of the heterosexual structure of marriage. The centrality of the romance narrative is announced by opening title cards which introduce the audience to a plurality of lesbian representations: 'This is Max.' 'These are Max's friends.' 'They try to cheer her up and fix her up.' These are followed by 'The story of a woman looking for Ms Right.' 'But going about it all wrong.' At this point the film seems to limit itself to the production of a lesbian reinterpretation of mainstream romance narrative, continuing the presumption that all a female audience desires, lesbian or not, are representations of the personal and the private. Such a narrowing of scope would ignore the public and historical problematics of lesbian identity, but such considerations are foregrounded in the very next scene. This takes place in a seminar room where Kia (Wendy Macmillan), an African American lesbian professor, asks the class to 'make a list of women you think or know are lesbians through history or present time'. The students come up with a small and varied list but question the authenticity or veracity of the names on it. Kia answers:

> Throughout lesbian history there is a serious lack of history to tell us what these women's lives are about. Lesbian lives and lesbian relationships barely exist on paper and it's that mindset and understanding of the meaning of history that we begin to want to change.

The representation of this pedagogical moment frames the romance narrative within the spoken desire for a retrieval of lesbian identity. This explicitly situates the film as part of this movement and offers the audience an inclusive position of 'we' to communally carry on this work. This doubling continues throughout the film, which uses the narrative tension of Max and Ely's relationship (will they/won't they get it together?) for a forward dynamic while intercutting scenes which question the constraining effects of such romance life narratives deriving from gay and mainstream culture.

For example, when Max and Ely return from their first date, a cinema visit, they are shown discussing the sexuality politics of the film they have just seen. The conversation has a similar effect to the earlier classroom scene in pointing out to the audience the difficulties in representing gay identity. Here the effect is even more self-reflexive since the focus of debate is the use of negative and positive representations in film and the responsibilities of the gay filmmaker. Because the conversation is handled in a realistic manner and the actual film is not named, the scene opens up a central debate about the construction of gay identity to a large audience in an unthreatening and non-divisive way, situating that audience with respect to that debate as they watch *Go Fish*. The discussion ends without acrimony and with a sense of both the desire for and the difficulty of producing a plurality of representations: 'I think we want him to represent everyone and he's just representing what he sees in the community.'

Go Fish continually stresses the plurality of its lesbian community in terms of ethnicity, profession and sexual behaviour. The film's representations of plural identities are focused around reactions to the romance narrative. The central romance of Max and Ely is decentred and critiqued in two main ways. First in its contrast to the relationships of central characters Kia and Daria (Anastasia Sharp), and second by a non-narrative meditation on marriage which represents Max's thoughts and fears surrounding heterosexuality. In the relationships of Kia and Daria the film shows 'positive' nurturing and 'negative' promiscuous images of lesbian coupling while at the same time demonstrating the problematics of desiring a stable, long-term relationship without identifying with heterosexist marriage.

In contrast to the hesitating shyness of Max and Ely, Daria's and Kia's affectional lives offer the audience alternative empathising positions. Kia's relationship with her partner, the Latina Evy (Migdalia Melendez), is represented as monogamous, long-term, loving and sexual. Daria is represented as serially monogamous. Each time the friends get together to discuss Max and Ely, Daria introduces them to a new girlfriend. At no time in *Go Fish* is disapproval of this mode of sexuality shown. It is only after Daria has sex with a man that disapproval is voiced. Stylistically, this episode is constructed to evoke images of gay bashing by heterosexuals. It is shot at night on a street with Daria isolated under a street lamp in front of a crowd of angry lesbians. Although actual physical violence is not represented the questioning of Daria is threatening. The crux of the dispute is whether Daria can be still be considered a lesbian though she has had heterosexual intercourse.

Daria counters accusations with 'I'm a lesbian who had sex with a man. If a gay man has sex with a woman he was bored, drunk, whatever. If a lesbian has sex with a man her whole life choice becomes suspect. I think that's suspect.' As with the earlier seminar and film discussion, this scene represents an ongoing and crucial debate about lesbian identity: how far is that identity based on a sex act, and if this is the only differentiating factor from mainstream society, are there no more positive and lesbian-specific elements to such an identity construction? Further, how far is this kind of demonising still reliant on the default position of heterosexual masculinity? As earlier, the film seems to be aligning lesbianism with a desire for a radical re-evaluation of the construction of sexual and gendered identity, against notions of internal policing. In this, *Go Fish* might be read as echoing the position articulated by critics such as Chris Straayer, who argues that:

> Lesbian 'deviance' refutes the all-encompassing 'natural' power of the male-female opposition as a defining principle. Lesbianism demands a new operation of subjectivity in which active desires, pleasures, and other specific declarations of identity construct a field of multiple entry points. Within this new operation, a heterosexual woman's active sexuality would not be consumed but empowered. Rather than enforcing two 'true' sexes, which allow one (male) subject, we must recognize the power of individual activities, in this case sexualities, to assert subjectivity.[45]

Go Fish confronts the continuing dominant power of this 'male-female opposition' in its representation of the institution of marriage. A sequence directly following Daria's interrogation suggests that the reaction against her act is governed by unexamined attitudes to marriage. Max is shown in a full white wedding dress with her voice-over imagining what it would be like to wake up and be married to a man. The voice-over emphasises the security and normalising force of the institution as it relates how she could be accepted as wife and mother in a family rather than left on the periphery as 'aunt', her lesbian past read as a 'phase' she has been saved from by a husband. As the voice constructs the recognisable pattern of a marriage her lesbian friends lift her wedding veil and kiss her. Next each of the main characters are shown wearing the dress, peeling it off and looking directly into camera. The segment closes with Max refuting the definition of lesbianism as an insubstantial phase and suggesting that such definitions are the result of a projected male heterosexual desire that can be countered: 'I'm not waiting for a man. We're not waiting for a man. I get this eerie feeling that a man's waiting for me.' The normative link between romance and the heterosexual structuring apparent in the institution of marriage is thus broken. This resituates radically the reworking of the romance motif in the film, producing innovative affectional relationships as the culmination of the diverse representations of lesbian identity discussed and shown in the movie. Therefore, though *Go Fish* ends with Max and Ely finally getting together this is not a resolution that relies on the approval of the heterosexual gaze or is grounded in heterosexual narratives.

Philadelphia: People like us?

The combined pressure of these 'new voices' and political activism can be seen as having elicited a response from Hollywood in the shape of Jonathan Demme's *Philadelphia*. As the project's working title 'People like us' suggests, this is a film directed at the mainstream and though it has been found wanting, specifically for its failure to represent fully the sexual relationship between the gay couple played by Tom Hanks and Antonio Banderas, it did bring a positive portrayal of gay identity to a national audience. As Richard Corliss remarked in *Time* magazine in respect of the film's success:

> America seemed to be accepting a few heretical notions: that a homosexual could earn respect and sympathy: that a star like Tom Hanks could play a gay man with credible grace: that another star, Denzel Washington, could play a homophobe who gets an education in brotherly love: that a film about AIDS could attract the mass audience thought to be hostile to films about the disease and its victims.[46]

As this implies, the reception of the film concentrated on the casting and the acceptance solicited by *Philadelphia* for the representation of gay identity as part of American identity.[47] Finally it seemed that the mainstream had accepted that gays were just like them. What we will examine here is how the film constructs this acceptance, and its reliance in this on the use of a negative stereotype of ethnicity and the stabilising force of the heterosexual gaze and images of the family.

Of course *Philadelphia* was not the first mainstream film to deal positively with gay identity and AIDS. *Longtime Companion* (1990) and the television movie *And the Band Played On* (Roger Spottiswoode, 1993) had both already represented the devastation wrought on gay communities by AIDS, the rise in homophobia and the lack of governmental reaction to the epidemic. *Longtime Companion* follows a group of white male gays, the death of two of them from AIDS-related illnesses and the politicisation of the remainder. The central relationship between David (Bruce Davidson) and Sean (Mark Lamos) is positively handled, especially when Sean becomes ill and dies, the melodrama of such scenes encouraging audience empathy. The personalising of the narrative of AIDS and the unthreatening representation of gay identity in these assimilable, white, middle-class and caring characters can all be seen to have influenced *Philadelphia*. However, though important as an antecedent, the representations of gay identity in *Longtime Companion* leave the mainstream viewer able to sympathise but not to articulate the interrelationship of identity construction and gay identity. It is an understanding of this relationship that *Philadelphia* can be seen to encourage.

As Demme and screenwriter Ron Nyswaner have both stressed, *Philadelphia* was made with the mainstream audience in mind. Demme told *Time* that 'I made this movie for people like me: people who aren't activists, people who are afraid of AIDS, people who have been raised to look down on gays.' [48] Hence the casting of Hanks in the role of Andrew Beckett, a positive stereotype of a white respectable professional lawyer. Hanks's previous roles in such family-orientated films as *Splash* (Ron Howard, 1984) and *Big* (Penny Marshall, 1988) were securely all-American, and emphasised the normativity of the character. As Hanks stated in *The Celluloid Closet* film, 'my screen persona is non-threatening. I've never been known to strike fear into anybody and because of this the idea of a gay man with AIDS is not scary.' Richard Corliss went still further in *Time*, heading his article on Hanks and his persona 'Hollywood's last decent man'.[49]

This desire to make the film hetero-friendly can be read throughout its length. The overall narrative of Hanks's dismissal due to discrimination by his law firm after the discovery of his HIV positive status situates the film within a recognisable courtroom genre picture. *Philadelphia* thus focuses on a fairly abstract and individualistic fight for justice which any audience can align themselves with, rather than representing the communal gay response to the lack of AIDS prevention. In fact, the film hardly represents the gay community as having any diversity. What there is – a scene outside the courtroom featuring gay and anti-gay groups of protesters – is very short and is quickly cut away to Washington in a bar. Later, the fancy dress party given by the Hanks and Banderas characters and Hanks/Beckett's wake take place within the safety of the domestic scene and are very obviously social rather than political gatherings. More screen time is given to showing Hanks/Beckett reassuringly large and overwhelmingly heterosexual family. The representation of the way in which this 'normal' family accept the gay partnership is an object lesson for the audience and of course naturalises the relationship. Thus at his parents' fortieth wedding anniversary when Hanks/Beckett explains the pressures which could result from the trial the family rally round to support him. During this conversation he is shown feeding a young baby while being embraced by Banderas. As well as the other family members providing a positive image of tolerance, the scene establishes audience sympathy and trust on the basis of the demonstration that Beckett and Miguel have the ability to replicate parenthood.

In this and many other ways the film is structured for the heterosexual gaze. The kinds of gay identity represented are white, male, professional and in couples, not communal, ethnically marked, leather-clad or lesbian. The spaces where these identities operate are the office, home, court and family, as opposed to the street and bars. As mentioned, contestation of general cultural homophobia is subsumed under Andrew Beckett's individual fight for justice. The main narrative and symbolic space for this dominant heterosexual position is created not through Beckett but via the figure of Joe Miller, the personal injury lawyer played by Denzel Washington. Washington's reactions as Miller, moving from hysterical fear and hatred of gays to legally representing Beckett and accepting his identity, is the frame through which the mainstream audience can judge their own reaction.

Producer Edward Saxon explained in *Esquire* magazine the centrality and function of Washington's role. The film needed a major straight character 'in part so the picture would find a wider audience, and in part to give people the feeling that their point of view was represented, including people who don't like homosexuals'.[50] As with Beckett's family, Miller is used to show the audience possible reactions to gays and AIDS, here a shift from homophobia to homophilia – even if only on an individual basis. This shift is easily readable from the contrasting of a number of key scenes. Miller's first reaction in hearing that Beckett has AIDS and has been sacked is to refuse the case. Having shook Beckett's hand he rushes to his doctor who tells him and therefore the audience that the HIV virus can only be transmitted 'through the exchange of bodily fluids'. Miller returns home to his wife and baby daughter where the full force of his homophobia and ignorance is represented in a conversation with the former: 'I don't want to be in bed with anyone who's stronger than me or has more hairs on his chest. You can call me old-fashioned, you can call me conservative, just call me a man.' This invocation of heterosexual masculinity as the natural default position is not approbated by his wife, but neither at this point in the film is there a countering argument. Even after he takes on the case Miller's homophobia continues, as for example in a bar scene, where he states he has only taken the case because the law firm has 'broken the law'. It is through the courtroom scenes that Miller's repositioning is effected. Shown to be frustrated by the refusal of witnesses to honestly admit Beckett's status as an exceptional lawyer he bursts out:

> You know, everyone in this courtroom is thinking about sexual orientation; who does what to whom and how they do it. Let's get it out in the open, out of the closet. Because this case is not just about AIDS; it's about the general public's hatred and loathing, fear of homosexuals and how that general feeling translated into his firing.

Thus Miller/Washington articulates the larger context, that the case is the result of national homophobia. Any part of the audience who has thus far been empathising with this figure must at this point decide either to follow him in supporting Beckett's case or to remain homophobic and align themselves with the unjust and unAmerican suppression of individual rights.

It is important to note that Miller's transformation is gradual and is framed by the security of his heterosexuality, thus reassuring straight audiences that their dominant position is not threatened. This can be exemplified by the represention of the fancy dress party given by Beckett and Miguel, and the following scene in which Hanks/Beckett listens to the opera singer Maria Callas. Miller is shown with his wife and at ease in a group of mixed sexuality. Both of the film's prominent couples are shot dancing (the scene shown in *The Celluloid Closet*) but the camera replicates the heterosexual couple's gaze, symbolically emphasising the dominance of their perspective. Directly after Hanks's peroration on Callas and love Miller is shown rushing home to his family, picking up his child and lying with his wife in bed. This is the only domestic shot of a couple in bed in the whole film and it carries the implicit message that heterosexual love is the only love. Significantly, the only portrayal of Miguel and Beckett in bed together takes place in hospital, on Beckett's deathbed.

We are not arguing that the structural use of Washington's character as a point of view for the audience is either unsuccessful or mistaken. In fact, it seems to be a highly propitious strategy. What is problematic is the film's use of his ethnicity and the lack of reaction to this use within the film and in its reception. In that his function is to represent hetero-sexuality it could be argued that the casting of an African American in this role is either irrelevant because white audiences would have no trouble in identifying with him, or it is reflective of the homophobia in the black community. However, it is precisely the specificity of Miller/Washington's ethnicity and the type of stereotype being invoked that allows the character to function as a stabilising force.

As we argued in our first chapter, the default position of white heterosexuality is no longer stable. Since visually Hanks as Beckett appears precisely to occupy that position, Miller/Washington's ethnicity visually represents sexualised difference and denotes the separate spheres of gay and straight. Of course, the irony is that here blackness is used to signal the mainstream which is usually read as white and heterosexual. But this ironic turn relies on a continued stereotyping of the black male as the extreme of heterosexual masculinity. Whereas in overtly racist representations this has worked as a negative stereotype with associations of barbarity and primitivism, here those associations have been amelior-ated but their symbolic invocation of the 'natural' is still central. What Miller's ethnicity and narrative encode then is first, that blackness and heterosexuality are natural, then that homophobic reaction to AIDS is 'natural', but that finally it can and should be overcome. The interrela-tionship of black and gay represented by Riggs has had to be suppressed. This is demonstrated in Miller's hysterical reaction to a gay black student who tries to pick him up in a drugstore. Unlike his initial homophobic treament of Beckett there is no balancing scene where Miller accepts black gay identity, and nor does the ideological economy of *Philadelphia* call for one. As with the film's rigidly heterosexual encoding of femi-ninity, a black gay identity must be disavowed since it would disturb its economy of race and sexuality.

In fact the film closes with that most innocent and natural signifier of American identity, childhood in the 1950s. At the post-funeral party the camera focuses on a home movie showing Beckett as a young boy in cowboy clothes playing with his siblings. Nostalgia is evoked by the use of the home movie and the time setting. This nostalgia for a moment before civil rights and before AIDS locates a lost America where the troubling identities of ethnicity and sexuality were not part of the national frame. As with the use of Washington's character, this is a reassuring narrative device for any audience: we are all the same, it suggests, because we have all been children. The differing historical situation of each individual childhood and their subsequent histories are subsumed in the normality of the cherubic and universalising image of the white middle-class child. Thus it would seem that even when the mainstream does positively represent a marginal group it can only be *one* group. The structuring paradigm of margins and centre remains dominant, and remains reliant on the absent and suppressed Other.

Notes

1. Vito Russo, *The Celluloid Closet: Homosexuality in the Movies* (New York: Harper and Row, 1981), p. 154.
2. Richard Dyer, 'Stereotyping', in Richard Dyer (ed.) *Gays and Film* (London: British Film Institute, 1977), pp. 27–39; p. 27.
3. Alan Sinfield, 'Diaspora and hybridity: queer identities and the ethnicity model', *Textual Practice* 10 (1996), pp. 271–93; p. 280.
4. Al LaValley, 'The great escape', in Corey K. Creekmur and Alexander Doty (eds), *Out in Culture: Gay, Lesbian and Queer Essays on Popular Culture* (London: Cassell, 1995), pp. 60–70; p. 60. Originally published in *American Film* 10/6 (April 1985); pp. 28–34, 70–1.
5. Russo, *Celluloid Closet*, pp. 188–9, 245–6.
6. LaValley, 'The great escape', p. 70.
7. Diana Fuss, 'Inside/Out', in Diana Fuss (ed.), *Inside/Out: Lesbian Theories/Gay Theories* (New York and London: Routledge, 1991), pp. 1–10; p. 2.
8. See *Baseline* entry on *Cinemania*.
9. Sinfield, 'Diaspora and hybridity', p. 271.
10. Sinfield, 'Diaspora and hybridity', p. 280 and passim; Edmund White, 'Gender uncertainties', *The New Yorker*, 17 July 1995, pp. 79–81; Didi Herman, 'The politics of law reform: lesbian and gay rights struggles into the 1990s', in Joseph Bristow and Angela R. Wilson (eds), *Activating Theory* (London: Lawrence and Wishart, 1993), pp. 251–2; Cindy Patton, 'Tremble, hetero swine', in Michael Warner (ed.), *Fear of a Queer Planet* (Minneapolis: Minnesota University Press, 1993), pp. 173–4; Corey K. Creekmur and Alexander Doty, 'Introduction', Creekmur and Doty, *Out in Culture*, pp. 1–11; p. 1.
11. Jonathan Ned Katz, *Gay American History: Lesbians and Gay Men in the USA* ([1976]; New York: Meridian, 1992, rev. edn); Karla Jay and Allen Young (eds), *Out of*

the Closets: Voices of Gay Liberation (London: GMP, 1992, twentieth-anniversary edition); Lilian Faderman, *Odd Girls and Twilight Lovers: A History of Lesbian Life in America* (Harmondsworth: Penguin, 1992).

12. Katz, *Gay American History*, p. 2.

13. Katz, *Gay American History*, p. 10.

14. Graffiti in the women's bathroom of the Lesbian and Gay Community Center, New York City, 1989. Andrea Weiss, *Vampires and Violets: Lesbians in the Cinema* (London: Jonathan Cape, 1992), p. 1.

15. Weiss, *Vampires and Violets*, p. 5.

16. Weiss, *Vampires and Violets*, p. 4.

17. Alexander Doty, *Making Things Perfectly Queer* (Minneapolis: University of Minnesota Press, 1993), p. 3.

18. Russo, *Celluloid Closet*, pp. 245–6.

19. Dyer, *Gays and Film*, p. 30.

20. David Meieran, 'Preface', in David Deitcher (ed.), *Over the Rainbow: Lesbian and Gay Politics in America Since Stonewall* (London: Boxtree, 1995), pp. 9–10.

21. Sylvia (Ray) Rivera in *The Question of Equality*; and in Deitcher, *Over The Rainbow*, p. 59.

22. Jewelle Gomez, 'Out of the Past', in Deitcher, *Over the Rainbow*, pp. 19–58; p. 25.

23. Bob Kohler, in *The Question of Equality*; and in Deitcher, *Over the Rainbow*, pp. 63–4.

24. Russo, *Celluloid Closet*, p. 248.

25. Russo, *Celluloid Closet*, p. 175.

26. Dyer, *Gays and Film*, p. 37.

27. *The Boys in the Band* (William Friedkin, 1970), quoted in Russo, *Celluloid Closet*, pp. 175–6 and excerpted in *The Celluloid Closet* film.

28. Gomez, 'Out of the past', p. 29.

29. Quoted in Henry Louis Gates, Jr., 'Blacklash?', *The New Yorker*, 17 May 1993, pp. 42–4; p. 44.

30. Henry Louis Gates, Jr., 'The black man's burden', in Gina Dent (ed.), *Black Popular Culture* (Seattle: Bay Press, 1992), pp. 75–83; p. 80.

31. Marlon Riggs quoted in Deitcher, *Over the Rainbow*, p. 95 (emphasis removed).

32. Valerie Smith, 'The documentary impulse in contemporary U. S. African-American film', in Dent, *Black Popular Culture*, pp. 56–64; p. 60.

33. Smith, 'The documentary impulse', p. 62.

34. Riggs quoted in Deitcher, *Over the Rainbow*, p. 94.

35. Mab Segrest, 'Visibility and backlash', in Deitcher, *Over the Rainbow*, pp. 79–116; pp. 96–101.

36. See Segrest, 'Visibility and backlash', pp. 104–5.

37. B. Ruby Rich, 'New queer cinema', *Sight and Sound* 2/5 (September 1992), pp. 31–4; p. 32.

38. Tom Kalin, 'Tom Kalin in conversation with Seun Okewole on "Swoon", style and desire', *Sight and Sound* 2/5 (September 1992), pp. 36–7; p. 37.

39. Amy Taubin, 'Beyond the sons of Scorsese', *Sight and Sound* 2/5, (September 1992), p. 37.

40. Kalin, 'In conversation', p. 36.

41. Taubin, 'Beyond', p. 37.

42. Weiss, *Vampires and Violets*, p. 163.

43. Cindy Patton, 'What is a nice lesbian like you doing in a film like this?', in Tamsin

Wilton (ed.), *Immortal Invisible: Lesbians and the Moving Image* (London: Routledge, 1995), pp. 20–33; p. 27.

44. Martha Gever, John Greyson and Pratibha Parmar (eds), *Queer Looks: Perspectives on Lesbian and Gay Film and Video* (New York and London: Routledge, 1993).

45. Chris Straayer, 'The hypothetical lesbian heroine in narrative feature film', in Creekmur and Doty, *Out in Culture*, pp. 44–59; p. 58.

46. Richard Corliss, 'The gay gauntlet', *Time*, 7 February 1994, pp. 62–4; p. 64.

47. See also for example Jennet Conant, 'Tom Hanks wipes that grin off his face', *Esquire* (December 1993), pp. 75–82, 146, and Richard Corliss, 'Hollywood's last decent man', *Time*, 11 July 1994, p. 58.

48. Quoted in Corliss, 'The gay gauntlet', p. 63.

49. Corliss, 'Hollywood's last decent man', p. 58.

50. Quoted in Conant, 'Tom Hanks', p. 80.

Conclusion: Aliens from
Star Wars to *Independence Day*

[silence] ... And that's all I've got to say about that.

> Forrest Gump on the Vietnam War, *Forrest Gump*
> (Robert Zemeckis, 1994)

Mankind, that word should have new meaning for all of us today. We can't be consumed by our petty differences any more. We will be united in our common interests. Perhaps it's fate that today is the fourth of July, and you will once again be fighting for our freedom, not from tyranny or persecution, but from annihilation. We are fighting for our right to exist. And should we win the day the fourth of July will no longer be known as an American holiday, but as the day the world declared we will not go quietly into the night. We will not vanish without a fight. We're going to live on. We're going to survive. Today we celebrate our Independence Day.

> Thomas J. Whitmore, President of the USA, *Independence Day*
> (Roland Emmerich, 1996)

One of the focal moments of the 1994 box-office sensation *Forrest Gump* is when the eponymous, low-IQ hero is asked to address an anti-war rally in the centre of Washington, DC on the subject of the Vietnam War. Just as Gump (Tom Hanks) begins to speak, the sound system is disabled and neither the onscreen nor the film audience hears what he has to say. When the sound is restored, all that is heard is 'and that's all I've got to say about that'. As we argued in our first chapter, *Forrest Gump* constructs American identity through the tropes of heterosexual romance and marriage, thereby suppressing the representation of histories of feminism, African American civil rights and gay liberation. Its marginalisation of these narratives and identities, like this speech, cannot be heard by the film's audience. *Forrest Gump* thus seems to have nothing to say about Vietnam, nor feminism, nor ethnicity, nor civil rights, nor sexuality. But of course, *Forrest Gump* actually has much to say about these things, concentrating 1960s counterculture in the characters of Gump's wife Jenny and his best friend and comrade in arms, Bubba. The death of both of these characters, the white hippie girl and the African American soldier, allows the film to strategically elide or to demonise representations of American identity that challenge the centrality of the straight white male.

Forrest Gump silences the politicisation of gendered, ethnic and sexualised identity because its articulation would disturb the stability of the film's construction of American identity as white, mainstream and heterosexual. Bubba's death in Vietnam not only particularises the war as individual tragedy rather than national failure or imperialist misadventure, but removes any need to show the post-Vietnam black struggle for civil rights except as the stereotyped violence of the Black Panthers. The transformation in the economic and ideological status of some African Americans propelled by the civil rights movement, and the continued privation of others, is absent. Instead, what is shown is the heroic Gump giving money to Bubba's mother, who hires a white servant for the family. This is the same kind of benevolent paternalism as that which we discussed in *Grand Canyon*. Jenny's narrative and death work similarly to position her as the structuring example of alternative politics and lifestyle. Her transition from naive hippie to drug abuser in the 1970s, and her death from an unnamed but AIDS-like disease suggests that this whole 1960s inheritance needs to die out, that family values must be re-established, that the countercultural threat from within deserves to die. In both cases reaction to these deaths is shown from Gump's point of view, and the audience can focus and empathise with his mourning. At the film's end they are left dwelling on the future of his child rather than the suppression of alternative identities.

If *Forrest Gump* works to nostalgically and silently homogenise American national identity, *Independence Day*, the box-office smash of 1996, does so loudly and jingoistically via its spectacular reworking of the alien movie. As the similarly successful re-release of *Star Wars* shortly afterwards allows us to see, in one sense Hollywood has come a long way from 1977 to 1996. In the *Star Wars* film of the first year, there is a simple binary split between white humanity and a range of strange and bizarre extraterrestrials. Nearly twenty years later in *Independence Day*, it is a multicultural (white, black, Jewish), male and female, though softly heterosexual USA that succeeds in repelling alien invasion. However, these multiculturalist credentials are established by acts of cultural imperialism, in the USA's assumption of global pre-eminence and, as the President's speech quoted above shows, by refashioning world history and identity into that of the USA.

This inspiring and war-mongering quotation, and the range of Ameri-can identities represented, demonstrates that in *Independence Day* the call to nationalism is the call to efface difference. The complexities of identity politics are reduced to 'petty differences'. Similarly to *Forrest Gump*, heterosexual coupling is used as a structuring trope for American identity, with the pre-battle marriage of Captain Steven Hillier (Will Smith) and Jasmine Dubrow (Vivica A. Fox) and the reconciliation of the estranged David Levinson (Jeff Goldblum) and Constance Spano (Margaret Colin). The threat here though is not from within, but from without: the aliens.

In a knowing reworking of Western motifs, the RV replacing the covered wagon, aliens replacing Native Americans, the full range of American identities are represented fighting on the same side. Stereo-typical qualities are reconfigured so that they become useful in the fight to preserve the American polity and human existence. Jewish cleverness is utilised to dismantle the aliens' defences, and the brute strength of black masculinity to punch them out. It seems that the aliens take the position of the structuring other that we have uncovered as a constant in recent American film. Therefore no American identity needs to be othered, or at least no ethnic identity.

The dominant trope of the film is the gendered separation of private and public. Men go to war and return victorious to the domestic sphere of the female. What allows the contact of men with men in the war scene to remain understood as heterosexual and not homosexual or homosocial (as in the gay hit *Top Gun*) are two major structuring moves. First, the knowing play on such films in a locker room scene early on, where the Will Smith character and his pilot buddy are caught in what looks to an incoming pilot like either a position of fellatio or of marriage proposal. Knowing that the ring is for Smith's fiancée the audience is positioned to enjoy the incident as a moment of disavowal. Second and more problematic is the death of the only discernible gay character in the film, Marty Gilbert (Harvey Fierstein). This camp/sissy character is engulfed by a fireball. In itself, the death of a gay character may be read as non-ideological (the President's wife also dies during the film), though it must recall to some extent the narratives of homosexuality and early demise described by Russo. However, Gilbert's death has further significance. Since he is the only identifiably gay character in the film, his exclusion from the victorious ethnic synthesis implies that *Independence Day* constructs homosexuality as remaining outside true Americanness.

This exclusion is confirmed by the troping of the aliens in terms of various homophobic constructions of homosexuality. They are sexually indeterminate, but are assumed to be male; they are destructive and apparently not heterosexually procreative; they are organic beings like 'us' but they are disabled by a (computer) virus. In a climactic moment, their mother ship is destroyed by being penetrated by a Vietnam veteran and one-time abductee, bellowing 'Hello boys, I'm back.' In spite of its multiculturalist model of American identity, then, *Independence Day* remains reliant on the paradigm of the structuring other. Even if heavily distanced through the imaging of the aliens, the need to identify this other by an act of exclusion persists.

One of the premises of this book has been a sense of the importance of discourses drawn from the traditions of identity politics in contemporary American film. It is apparent from the examples discussed here that across mainstream, marginal, liberal, radical, right and left, similar structures of centre and margin persist. The move from *Star Wars* through *Forrest Gump* to *Independence Day* shows that in American culture the resolution of difference remains an ongoing project, capable of multiple resolutions in the service of different politics, but one that remains continually problematised by a structuring otherness.

Index

The British Association for American Studies (BAAS)

The British Association for American Studies was founded in 1955 to promote the study of the United States of America. It welcomes applications for membership from anyone interested in the history, society, government and politics, economics, geography, literature, creative arts, culture and thought of the USA.

The Association publishes a newsletter twice yearly, holds an annual national conference, supports regional branches and provides other membership services, including preferential subscription rates to the *Journal of American Studies*.

Membership enquiries may be addressed to the BAAS Secretary, Philip John Davies, Reader in American Studies, School of Humanities, De Montfort University, Leicester LE1 9BH, UK.